Writing Down Music

Writing Down Music

ALAN BOUSTEAD

LONDON
OXFORD UNIVERSITY PRESS
NEW YORK TORONTO
1975

Oxford University Press, Ely House, London W.1

GLASGOW   NEW YORK   TORONTO   MELBOURNE   WELLINGTON
CAPE TOWN   IBADAN   NAIROBI   DAR ES SALAAM   LUSAKA   ADDIS ABABA
DELHI   BOMBAY   CALCUTTA   MADRAS   KARACHI   LAHORE   DACCA
KUALA LUMPUR   SINGAPORE   HONG KONG   TOKYO

ISBN 0 19 317104 X

© *Oxford University Press 1975*

Printed in Great Britain
by Ebenezer Baylis & Son Limited
The Trinity Press, Worcester, and London

Contents

PART II: PRACTICE

Introduction

Music is a means of communication; for its sounds to be continually realized it needs to be recorded in some way. In fact the only way this can be satisfactorily done is for it to be written down; other possible methods (gramophone recording, sound graphs, etc.) are either not sufficiently accurate, or too complex to convey the correct message to the performer.

The responsibility for writing down in an accurate and clear manner rests in the first instance with the composer. Yet how many established composers writing today can honestly claim that as students they received a proper training in committing their ideas to paper? Most will admit that they had little more than a professorial reprimand—'your manuscript is appalling!' —and were left to discover the mysteries of the art for themselves from printed copies.

To present an entirely correct, unambiguous page should obviously be the aim of everyone who commits pen to music paper. It is true that the composer's finally printed copy has probably had the assistance of an army of editors, proofreaders, engravers, copyists, and more. But with the observance of a few simple rules and the taking of a little care in writing a page of music, their work can be cut to a minimum; the simple, obvious error and, worse, ambiguity can easily be avoided.

Composers, arrangers, and professional copyists may be regarded as specialists in writing down music, as they have to do it more or less continually. If even they have not been given a proper training in the rules governing the setting out of a page of music (and many have not, but have acquired the knowledge through experience), it is most unlikely that the performer, teacher, librarian, or any one else who has to write music just occasionally will have had such a training. The humble ninth extra trumpeter amending an orchestral part, or the class music teacher copying a melody on to the blackboard, needs to do it accurately, legibly, and correctly for it to have any value. The exactness required from this latter group is no less than that required from the professional copyist; in fact, throughout this book references to copyists include all those who have to copy music occasionally, as well as full-time professionals.

Good score-writing and good copying are easily achieved by the application of sound common sense to the accepted rudiments of music. It might seem, therefore, that the need for this book does not exist; but it is a fact that in reading music, as in reading words, the craftsmanship which has gone into the preparation of the page is taken for granted. The eye may spot an error (if the mind does not automatically correct it), but neither eye nor mind is trained to register what is right with a page.

A composer who writes an untidy, or even inaccurate score is unlikely to receive performances, unless he is well established; and the well-established composer who does write an untidy, inaccurate score is very rare. Many scores of the works of great composers can be studied in facsimile; those of Bach, Verdi, and Wagner, for example, combine an admirable clarity with individual characteristics; even Mozart in a hurry and the much maligned Beethoven, whose intensity seems to burst from the pen-nib, remain clear in their intentions and instructions. Nevertheless, the young composer's score is often both untidy and inaccurate and full of examples of broken rules. Conductors, performers, and adjudicators are unlikely to give much, if any, of their time to such a score, and there is no reason why they should. Ensembles and soloists are not likely to spend their time rehearsing works in which the prime difficulty is deciphering the pages before them. Even if he does not put his score directly before the conductor and performer, and employs the talents of a copyist, the composer can hardly expect an accurate translation of what he himself has failed to provide.

The copyist, alas, almost always places his work directly before the performer; his need for the utmost clarity and accuracy cannot be overstressed. One single wrong note can easily cost a minute of rehearsal time, and the cumulative effect of this can easily be imagined and is, regrettably, occasionally experienced. A rehearsal should be for learning the right notes of a piece, not deciphering them and correcting wrong ones. The waste of time and money the latter case involves, not to mention the fraying of even the mildest temperaments, is not likely to be the background to a good performance. The composer with the badly written score is likely to remain unknown; the copyist who produces untidy, unhelpful parts is not likely to be asked again.

Such a state of affairs, however, is easily avoided. It is no more difficult to write a tidy score than an untidy one, or to copy well than badly. After the necessary rules become second nature, producing bad work becomes the more difficult of the two. It will not be possible to reproduce a page resembling fine engraving, not at least without spending an enormous amount of time and using a large number of additional drawing instruments and other aids. It is an ideal worth keeping in mind, however, and by taking a little care and forethought the humble pen and ink can be used to produce a satisfactorily clear and accurate alternative. A good musical hand is not difficult to acquire; as with handwriting of words little more is needed than a knowledge of the components, the language, and plenty of practice. Spacing, however, plays a greater part in the layout of music, as do corrections (one cannot simply cross out an error), and a comparison with the written word-pictures of the oriental languages is more appropriate. The exact placing in these of each and every line affects the meaning of the resulting character, as the exact placing of each musical symbol or component affects the sound produced.

Despite all mechanical aids available to the writer of words, the composer of music still writes his score by hand, without any such help. (This excludes excursions into the world of electronic sounds, but a case can be made for this being a different subject altogether.) His essential needs, apart from a knowledge of his subject and a few basic writing materials, are clarity, accuracy, and speed, none of which may be sacrificed to the needs of the others. The need for clarity and absolute accuracy can easily be felt by imagining oneself on the receiving end of the work involved. Speed, which is almost synonymous with money to composer, arranger, and—even more—professional copyist, need not affect the other two requirements. One soon becomes sufficiently experienced to know how much work one can take on in a given amount of time. The copyist in particular should learn reluctantly to refuse last-minute scores that will involve over-rushing his work; he will not be thanked for the resulting lowered standard.

Throughout the following pages a number of rules and regulations will appear. These are accepted as more or less mandatory for engravers, etc., for whom this book is not intended. The writer of music manuscript should also adopt them, almost without relaxation. The occasional circumstance will arise when this will affect the clarity of the work involved, but this will be far less often than may at first be expected. Permissible deviations from the rules will be dealt with in the text at the appropriate moments.

Musical notation is inadequate at the best of times and cannot even express a genuine rubato (neither, for that matter, can a printed play text exactly define a vocal inflection). It is neither possible nor desirable to notate accurately what is often called the 'romantic' style of piano playing, in which the left hand frequently precedes the right in passages notated to be played simultaneously. Nevertheless the 'mathematics' of the art of music are readily understood by both composer and performer (it is to be hoped) and any departure from them needs very sound reasons to be accepted as an improvement rather than a 'quirk'.

In judging one's own musical hand a spirit of self-criticism is always necessary; for, like handwriting, it is comprehensible to the writer because he is familiar with it. The performer or reader may not be so familiar. The young composer who recently declared at a public conference that he wrote only for himself and cared not for his performers and audience (and was immediately censured by the eminent conductor on the same panel), need not presumably write down anything at all. Those of us who are concerned with communicating, however, must always attempt to achieve at least the clarity and un-ambiguity of the best printed page.

Part I: Principles

CHAPTER ONE
Essential Materials

Pen, ink, paper, a straight-edge, and an eraser, are the essential tools. To these may be added any number of available aids, until the point is reached at which freehand is entirely eliminated, the process of 'writing' has become an act of draughtsmanship, and the result is an architectural design which, although perfectly satisfactory, is beyond the province of this book.

Paper

Scores and copies of single parts which are required once only, or are not likely to be required for simultaneous rehearsals or performances in different places, should be written on ordinary opaque manuscript paper—as also will be such things as composers' sketches, students' exercises, etc. The three common sizes of paper are folio (36×27 cm.), quarto (31×24.5 cm.), and octavo (25×17.5 cm.). For most general purposes the quarto size is the most convenient: the octavo size has little practical use except for chorus parts. There are variations within these sizes—the given measurements are only approximate—and paper used for scoring for large orchestra may be considerably larger, its size being to a large extent governed by the number of staves printed on it.

The texture of the paper should be firm, the surface matt and neither shiny nor greasy, as the two latter qualities have an unhappy association with ink. A soft-textured paper will almost certainly cause the ink to feather.

The number of staves printed on a normal quarto sheet will usually be ten or twelve. It has been my own experience that it is almost impossible to produce a clearly detailed, well written page of music on a twelve-stave quarto sheet unless the music is extremely inactive and well confined between the outer stave lines. Anyone doubting this is advised to try the following experiment. On such a twelve-stave sheet write the note G of an open violin string, and beneath it add the dynamic f. On the line immediately below write the note E an octave above the open string, and above it add the down-bow sign. Without the addition of any further markings of tempo, phrasing, etc., the two lines will already be running into each other, and this is by no means an extreme case of notation. Advance planning to avoid this sort of disaster will be dealt with later. But a fundamental rule is that if one cannot plot a line parallel to the stave lines between the events of one stave and the next, then the best ruling of paper has not been chosen.

A stave ruling of 8 mm. in width, with a space of 2 cm. between staves, will be found ideal for almost all uses, except perhaps an extremely florid flute or violin solo part, when it might become necessary to leave a blank stave between lines of music. I have recently been using an eight-stave ruling in such instances, with the same depth of stave but a space of 2.8 cm. between them. Though at first this may seem a little extravagant it does allow eight staves to a page instead of a possible five only (leaving blank ones) on a ten-stave paper. The measurements given above allow ten staves to be printed comfortably on a quarto page and twelve on a folio page, and are strongly to be recommended.

Transparent papers, for dyeline reproduction (see p. 12), should of course be identical in ruling. The surface of the paper will naturally be hard, but again qualities of shine and grease have the same bad effects on ink, and make satisfactory reproduction impossible. Too thick or heavy a paper will not give a uniformly good print, since it diffuses the light in the exposure process, and thin or lightweight paper will curl under heat, and even under ordinary handling, with disastrous results. The best medium grade of paper is a natural tracing paper weighing about $90g/m^2$; this will also allow corrections to be made without unduly affecting the surface.

All work on transparent paper is done on the other side to that on which the lines are printed. There are two basic reasons for this; firstly, the printed lines will affect the even distribution of the ink of anything drawn through them. (A few experiments will show the extent of this.) Secondly, any erasure can be made if necessary, without affecting the printed lines in any way.

After a little experimenting it should be possible to find papers, both opaque and transparent, which exactly suit one's own hand. If one is using paper in any quantity, it is unquestionably a considerable advantage to have both types made to personal specification. Any ruling is then constantly available, the texture is familiar, and the quantity cost is no more than having to buy regularly the odd quire of paper in whatever ruling happens to be available. This last practice invariably produces a study full of odd sheets of unused paper, none of which matches any other in texture or ruling. A small stock of both twenty and twenty-four stave paper is also useful, except for the composer regularly writing for large orchestra, who will need more. Here the staves will of necessity be printed closer together, and probably narrower; a width of 6 mm. and a space of 8 mm. would seem to be at once acceptable and a practical minimum. The problems of other rulings should be tackled as they arise.

One of the enormous advantages the engraver has over the writer by hand is that his stave-lines are not pre-ruled, so he can vary the distance between staves as demanded by the music on them. The humble scribe is indeed slave to his paper, with its equidistant rulings, which remain the same whether he is writing pages of silent bars or the most virtuoso of duets for piccolo and tuba. It will more than repay him to give some time and thought to the selection of his materials.

Pens and Pencils

A certain amount of experiment with various shapes of nib is recommended to find what is best suited to one's own style. A few essentials should be borne in mind. The best nib is that which will make a thin downward stroke and a thicker horizontal one under the same light pressure—the majority of musical symbols having these characteristics. Under increased pressure the prongs should open slightly to give thicker lines, but the construction and material of the nib should be sufficiently strong to resist such pressure. The manipulation necessary to guide a very flexible nib is exhausting to the hand and finger muscles. It should not have the reinforced tip often found on fountain pen nibs, since this tends to even out the thickness of the stroke in any direction; a two-pronged nib is sufficient, the additional properties of a third prong being unnecessary. A nib fitted with a reservoir attachment for holding the ink is so great an asset as to be an essential. Not only does it make constant dipping unnecessary, but it also virtually eliminates the danger of blotting.

A second pen fitted with a finer nib, though still possessing the other qualities mentioned, will be found useful for ruling lines, since the pressure against the ruler tends to open the prongs of the 'standard' nib further than usual to produce an unnecessarily thick line. It will also be found useful for writing grace-notes and any other details which need to be smaller and finer (this might even include a sung text).

Nibs should always be kept clean, and any clogged, dried ink removed regularly to prevent corrosion. A clogged pen, if it will write at all, will make characters much thicker and more irregular than those intended. (Clogging is particularly difficult to spot in fountain pen sacs.) Any good ink solvent will take care of this, but it is just as easy to clean a good steel nib under a running water-tap, and pare off the dried ink with a razor blade, carefully avoiding damage to the nib (or finger-tips).

Although fountain pens specifically for music writing are available, hand-dipped penholders and nibs are easier to clean and change, and do seem generally more flexible; their construction also makes working with a straight-edge or ruler easier. In either event the choice of holder will again be a personal matter, though in no circumstances should it be too thin. My own dip-penholder is a tapered round shape about 12 mm. in diameter at the gripping end, with part of the circle levelled off. This flat surface rests alongside the fingertip joint of the second finger and is gripped there by the natural locking positions of thumb and first finger. This position allows all the flexibility desired with the minimum of actual movement. It is true, however, that this particular grip may not suit all hands. Some might also consider my penholder on the thick side, though it does not seem to me to be much thicker than the average fountain pen, and its slightly heavier weight is an advantage in controlling its movement.

The principles of the ball-point pen make it unsuitable for use in writing music manuscript, though it has one valuable asset which will be mentioned shortly. Pens designed for the drawing office are similarly unsuitable since they produce characters of constant thickness, though they can be an asset for ruling bar lines, adding texts, etc.

Pencils should be used for rough work only, such as sketching, and perhaps in the classroom, where the provision of special pens and inks is not a practical proposition. Well shaped characters are far more difficult to form with a pencil, and pencilled work on the music stand has a tendency to reflect the light or even become invisible. The best grade is a B or 2B, and a blunted chisel-shaped sharpening more satisfactory than a point.

Ink

Ink should be true black for all music writing (not blue-black). The use of coloured inks is not recommended. Even for rehearsal lettering or cueing they are a time-consuming conceit; they do not reproduce well at all, and in any case they do not reproduce in colour. Take warning from the composer who recently corrected his score in red ink, and then had a photocopy made and sent to a copyist. The accompanying instructions about notes in red were, of course, meaningless!

For writing on opaque papers any good quality ink, preferably containing a solvent, is satisfactory. For writing on transparent papers a heavier ink is necessary to obtain the best density for reproduction. Most Indian inks are too strong and will constantly clog the pen nib; they draw the surface of the paper together as they dry; and they also tend to dry too thickly for a clean erasure to be made. A drawing ink of the type suitable for fountain pens (e.g. Rotring Fount India) is best. It gives a satisfactory blackness, and may also be erased without damage to the paper.

Erasers

That highly specialized piece of equipment, the electric eraser, is a luxury most writers can manage without, whatever its value to the orchestral librarian. Some type of eraser is essential, however; even the perfectionist who never makes a mistake (and incidentally doesn't exist) may be called upon to correct somebody else's copy. The most simple and effective eraser is a sharp razor blade, always to be treated with the utmost respect. Add to this a fibre-glass eraser (of the type similar in design to a propelling pencil, for which refills are available) and a soft pencil rubber, and all errors can be taken care of.

The procedure for making corrections on opaque and transparent papers varies slightly, and will in any case depend on the extent of the error. The first point to decide is whether the time spent on making the correction is not going to be longer than beginning the page anew. On opaque papers the best method of dealing with a substantial error is to write the correct version on a separate sheet of paper, cut round it leaving a small margin and then tape or paste it over the incorrect portion. Use no more tape or glue than is absolutely necessary. (A 'double-sided' tape gives the best results.) It is obviously easier to begin such a correct 'insert' at the beginning of a line and end at the end of a line to avoid having to cut a jigsaw pattern. This method will probably be the only one possible in correcting a longish part in book form.

For smaller corrections the error should be blotted if noticed immediately, but in any case the correct version should be written in first if it involves only a few symbols. This should be allowed to dry naturally. Then with the razor blade and the gentlest of pressures gradually remove the error and as little of the surface of the paper as possible. A pin-point accuracy is possible with a razor blade which cannot be achieved with the regular type of 'ink-rubber'. Any necessary touching-up of stave lines, note-stems etc., is best done with a ball-point pen: regular ink will feather across the damaged strands of the paper surface and might make an ugly blot.

A substantial error on a transparency is almost always best dealt with by recopying. It is possible to cut out the incorrect passage and splice in a correct version using an 'invisible' adhesive tape; no overlapping of the paper is permissible as this will appear as a black area in the reproduction (having doubled the density of the paper). Some evidence of a splicing almost always shows in reproduction. Again a small error should be blotted if noticed at once, to take up as much ink as possible. When the surrounding part is completely dry a light rubbing with a fibre-glass eraser will completely remove the ink and leave the surface comparatively unharmed. Before writing the correct version the surface should first be cleaned with a soft rubber, otherwise the ink will feather around the small pieces of fibre-glass. Care should be taken not to brush these away with the hand, as one does after using a pencil rubber. The minute splinters will almost certainly lodge in the skin, and although not dangerous they are certainly very irritating.

The very smallest errors can be removed with a razor blade. If the area is to be written over again, it is best to clean the surface with a soft rubber first; this will have the effect of restoring some of the smoothness to the surface.

I would recommend practice in these methods, in order to appreciate the processes involved and to gain experience, before having to apply the knowledge in the midst of a complex page. They are sufficient to cover all contingencies, and although it is possible, for example, to remove an error while still wet with a razor blade and insert the correction immediately, this sort of act requires a degree of confidence not always repaid by the result.

Rulers

Either a ruler or a straight-edge is necessary for coping with lines too long for freehand. It should have a raised edge to avoid ink-smudging. Those made of metal keep their edges longer, but are more prone to slipping than plastic ones. Two will be found useful; a long one of about 40–45 cm., mostly for use on large scores, and a small 15 cm. one for all other work. The edges should be cleaned of ink regularly.

Blotting Paper

This has two uses only; immediate blotting of an error to take up as much ink as possible, and as a guard to protect the paper from the hand during writing. Oils from the skin will otherwise affect the paper before it is written on, with a resulting poor distribution of ink. All correctly written work should be allowed to dry naturally for the best results, and never blotted.

Backing Sheet

A good backing sheet on which to rest the work page is essential: writing on a sheet of paper directly backed by a desk or tabletop will have an adverse effect on both paper and table. A large, heavy sheet of manuscript paper is best (this may be rested on a sheet of cardboard for further protection), since the stave lines will show through a sheet of transparent paper and can be used as a guide for anything needing to be written outside the stave. A few bar lines ruled on the backing sheet will also help considerably with alignment.

Aids beyond these few are varied and numerous; they are for personal investigation, and rejection or adoption as one sees fit. Any aid, however, which is time-consuming in its use is likely to be a hindrance. The materials dealt with above, used in conjunction with a good hand, are all that is necessary for all work except that intended as a master copy for publication.

Other Requirements

To make the most of these materials and one's talents good working conditions are essential. A steady table is required, with a hard flat surface wide enough to hold the sheets of paper being worked on, and also perhaps a book-rest and a table lamp. Some particular, regular place of work should be found in every home, however small; nobody's best work is done on the kitchen table surrounded by the washing-up. If copying I personally prefer to have the work being copied flat on the table also, rather than on a book-rest, thus reducing the up and down movement of head and eyes, and also making it possible to keep a guiding finger on the original if it is very complex. Natural daylight can come from either left or right, as it throws no shadows of any importance unless it is blocked. Direct sunlight however, should be avoided; it is harmful to both work and worker. Artificial light throws strong shadows and should therefore come from the left (to the right-handed). My own preference, though, is for an adjustable angle-lamp, with the beam directed closely to the original work; the attendant spill of light is exactly sufficient for working in.

A comfortable, armless chair at the right height is indispensable. If it is the wrong height, this will soon make itself felt;

for if it is too high the shoulder muscles will soon protest, and if it is too low an aching back will result. In any case sitting at the writing desk for longer than two hours without moving the rest of the body is not recommended. In that period maximum concentration and speed will have been attained. Although at first it may seem foolish to break into such a flow, after a five minute rest (or exercise) away from the desk this ideal state is quite quickly re-achieved and maintained. But continuing for much more than two hours without a break brings on a rapid decline in efficiency. This is a ruling easily adopted by the copyist, though of course it may not always suit the student writing an exercise for the following morning, or the composer writing on the full tide of inspiration.

Finally a word about the surrounding decor. Too much white will be found to be a great strain on the eyes. True, manuscript paper is white, though a pale-coloured backing sheet to a transparent sheet is always to be preferred. But transferring one's gaze to the soft colours of trees and grass beyond the window—if one is so fortunate as to be able to do so—should take place fairly often, and probably will automatically. A soft-coloured wall is to be preferred to white, if one has the choice; blotting paper, which will always be present on the work table, need never be white; plenty of alternative colours are available (pale green is ideal).

Heat and, alas, too much comfort are sleep-inducing.

Methods of Reproduction

Not so many years ago, if many copies of a part were required (e.g. ten violin parts) they were all individually copied, one after another—and therefore all liable to variation. The rapid advances of reproduction techniques have now made it possible to have any number of copies made from a single master copy.

It has of course always been possible to photograph an ordinary page of music, prepare an auto-positive, and make copies from this, or even make an instantly usable copy (e.g.

Xerox). The results, however, are never totally satisfactory from a player's point of view, though as a method of reproducing a score it is still in use, and its appearance not unacceptable. The most widely used, simple, and satisfactory method of music reproduction (as opposed to the expensive business of printing) is the dyeline method.

Though its technicalities need not concern us, it is necessary to understand its basic principles in order to produce the best master copies. The master copy is written on a transparent sheet of paper, with the stave lines already printed; writing is done on the other side of the paper, for reasons which have been explained. The copy is made using a heavy black ink (not an ordinary water ink) and this master is then put through a machine which makes a direct exposure on sensitized paper. This is then set or fixed, and any number of copies can be made from it. It follows that any variation in the density of the writing affects the amount of light which can or cannot pass through the blackness of the notes on the master copy; this in turn will give rise to variations in the reproductions from an acceptable dense black to a very disturbing near-invisible faintness. The lesson to be learnt here is to use the right quality of ink and to keep the pen well filled with it.

CHAPTER TWO

Basic Symbols

In writing music by hand the symbols used by long-established publishing houses should be copied as far as possible. An exception may be made in the case of the C clef and the crotchet rest, both of which are too elaborate in their detail to be copied quickly. But it is no excuse to write stems on the wrong side of the noteheads or tails on the wrong side of the stems merely because it is quicker, any more than it is to write the letter *d* instead of *b* for the same reason. Any method, right or wrong, can be accomplished with satisfactory speed after sufficient practice; it is far better to begin and persevere with correct imitations of the printed symbols than to invent alternatives.

Clefs and Signatures

It is important to remember that the three common clef signs, G, F, and C, indicate the position of these respective notes on the stave. The G or treble clef has a central curl around the second line up on the stave. It is easier to begin with this curl, since the alternative involves making an upward vertical stroke, the most difficult with pen and ink. The tip and the tail extend beyond the stave lines; the curve on the tail is sometimes omitted, but since making it automatically brings the pen back to the stave, nothing is gained by this omission.

The shape of the C clef varies from hand to hand, the printed version not being easily written quickly. The version shown here is both immediately recognizable and made in the minimum time. Note that since the two arms enclose middle C, the alto clef is contained within the stave lines, while the tenor clef is a space higher.

The F or bass clef is usually contained within the top four lines of the stave. The two small dots surrounding the line for the note F should not be omitted (these were once also used in conjunction with the treble clef, though this practice is now obsolete).

Key signatures, when appropriate, follow the clef, and are written in the accepted order of rising sharps and descending flats, with displacements which are often misunderstood in the alto and tenor clefs. The following table shows the positions of all seven sharps and flats in all four clefs, from which the correct placing for any key signature may be seen. Clefs and key signatures (but not time signatures) should appear at the beginning of every stave of music; the practice of writing a clef and signature on the first line of the page only is to be avoided.

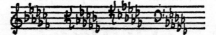

Time signatures follow key signatures, if any. On single staves they are written through the stave; for two-stave instruments they should be written similarly through each stave. The laborious process of writing the same signature thirty times in a full score of thirty lines can be avoided in several ways (see Chapter 9). The dividing line, as in fractions, sometimes seen between the figures is a misconception and should not be used. Some 'modern' methods of writing time signatures as shown here have no special value and are invariably retranslated to the accepted standard method by players.

Changes in Clef, Key, and Time

A clef is changed for convenience of reading; the new clef should be placed immediately before the first note to which it applies, unless this note is a fraction of the smallest unit of the bar and follows a rest; in this case the new clef precedes the rest. The normal clef of an instrument should be restored as soon as possible, at the end of a bar, even if rests follow.

Key signature changes are usually—though not necessarily—preceded by a double bar line, which need have no significance other than to draw attention to the change. It is only necessary to write the new signature; the practice of first cancelling the old one with naturals is not necessary, and often confusing, as a change from E flat minor to F sharp major will show.

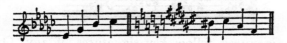

If the new section has no signature, however, cancellation with naturals is obviously necessary.

Time signature changes should be written immediately following a bar line; a double bar is not a necessity, though one will often appear for other reasons; in a piece with many changes of time the use of a double bar line is both time-consuming and confusing.

All changes which affect the beginning of a new line should also be noted at the end of the previous one, clef changes before the bar line, key signature and time changes after it.

The following example, though unlikely in musical terms, displays all the points so far mentioned.

It will be seen that the time change involving a new unit, in this case ⅔ to ⅝, should also include a note above the bar in which it occurs showing the relationship between the new and old value. Where the quaver remains constant in length this is shown by ♪=♪ ; where a new value is required ♩=♩. is written. The 'equals' sign should be placed exactly over the bar line, with the respective units on the sides to which they relate (see (a) below). No other indication is necessary; arrows, which are sometimes added, contribute nothing. If the change occurs between two systems it is shown as at (b) below. Other methods shown at (c) can give rise to confusion.

Accidentals

Accidentals should fully embrace the same line or space as the note to which they refer, and are easily drawn in the following manner. For sharps the two vertical lines should be drawn first, the right hand one slightly higher placed than the left; the two shorter lines across should then be made, rising slightly from left to right. The resulting enclosed space should be just sufficient to enclose a note-head. As with most musical symbols, the horizontal members should be a little thicker than the vertical ones, but a good pen nib, as already described, will take care of this without any effort by the writer. The flat should not too closely resemble the lower-case type 'b'; the rounded member, drawn second, is tapered towards the bottom and is more half-heart-shaped than half-round. There are many ways of making a natural sign, but the method of drawing two joined hooked strokes does not give a well angled centre, which should be identical to that of a sharp. I would recommend the order of strokes to be: left vertical, upper inclined horizontal and right vertical combined (with a strongly angled joint), finally closing the shape with a parallel stroke to the upper one. As with the sharp, the pen will automatically take care of the thickness required. The double sharp is merely a cross, with members about one and a half stave spaces deep; the double flat is simply two ordinary flats side by side, the practice of beaming the tips not being recommended.

The final part of the above example shows a careless application of an accidental only too often found in a manuscript score; it could be either A♭ or B♭, or, if this sort of carelessness abounds in the writing, almost anything.

An accidental lasts only for the bar in which it appears, unless its note is tied over the bar line. If the note appears again after such a tie either the accidental must be repeated or its cancellation used, whichever is appropriate. It is a not uncommon, and often helpful, practice to cancel an accidental in a bar immediately following its use.

If a note with an accidental is tied from one line to the next the accidental is sometimes repeated in brackets. The adoption of this method is optional; it will be found to be space-consuming, and quite difficult to write when applied to tied chords with many accidentals; it does, however, have a safety value. If employed, it must be used consistently through the copy.

Composers writing atonal scores (and those copying them) in which accidentals apply only to the notes they precede should state the fact clearly at the beginning of their scores (or parts). This practice, however, does little more than confuse by its defiance of convention, and is of little value except in unmeasured sections. (See Chapter 12.)

As with changes of key, a new accidental applied to a note does not require any previous one to be cancelled.

In part-writing all accidentals must be applied to the same side of all note-heads; this will be easily achieved if the note-heads are properly placed in the first instance.

Accidentals before chords should be written in ascending order, alternating left and right positions as required by spacing. A displaced second may affect this pattern, however.

A number of symbols have been used by composers to denote quarter tones (and three-quarter tones), some of which are given in the following example. They are all easily misread, however, when included with traditional accidentals. For the sake of clarity I would recommend an arrow joined to the note-head in the opposite direction to the stem. This will limit the choice of notation in certain instances.

Safety Accidentals

Accidentals which are not strictly 'grammatically' necessary, but included as a safety measure, should be kept to an absolute minimum. They have particular value in notating a 'false' octave, an unusual chord, and when a change takes place immediately in a new bar.

But accidentals placed before every note (and therefore mostly natural signs) are not only time- and space-consuming, but confusing and difficult to read.

The practice of bracketing them if they must be used, and therefore taking still more space, should be avoided; if they are thought to be necessary they should not be so modestly apologetic. An exception occurs in editions of old music, where the convention is often that a normal accidental is in the original, a small one is an editorial addition, and a bracketed one is cautionary only. Though a necessity for the scholar, these distinctions are not an aid to the player in actual performance.

Rests

All shapes follow the printed pattern and are easy to reproduce, with the exception of the crotchet rest. The older style of reversed quaver rest is confusing used in conjunction with other rests, and should be discarded; an extended variation however is immediately recognizable, and either this or an alternative simpler version of the printed symbol should be adopted and maintained.

Rests of longer duration than a semibreve are now only rarely encountered, particularly as the semibreve rest does duty for a full bar's rest in any time-signature. Care should be taken always to distinguish clearly between the semibreve rest, which hangs from the fourth stave line up, and the minim rest, which sits on the third line. The following example shows the positioning on the stave of most of the rests in general use. Note particularly the placing of the curves for rests of a quaver duration and less.

In handwritten music it is not uncommon to find these latter rests contracted as shown; although contrary to engraving practice, this is permissible provided clarity is maintained.

Parts sharing a stave need individual rests, which must be appropriately displaced, except when the same value of rest will serve both parts; it is then placed in its usual position.

Dotted rests should be used only in compound time (but see Compensating Rests, p.22). A rest of several bars'

duration is expressed by an extended semibreve rest with the relevant number of bars placed either above or just cutting into the stave (but not below). In two-stave parts the figure is placed between the staves. It is not necessary to fill the stave with a collection of rest symbols adding up to the number concerned.

Compensating Rests

Rests which complete a beat, a natural division of a bar, or a whole bar if there is no natural division left, should not be of longer duration than the note they immediately follow. This rule is often misapplied in compound time.

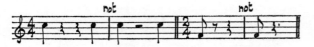

Having observed the rule, the longest available rest should be used.

The only exception to the above is that the following example is becoming standard practice, and is also usable with shorter notes and rests (but not longer ones). It should be avoided in compound time.

It will be seen that this also goes against the ruling of no dotted rests in simple time, but I do not find this single instance either offensive or misleading.

Notes

In all cases the note-head should be of a size to fill the space between two stave lines, and must remain constant in size; a variety of sizes makes reading difficult. The best actual shape for a note-head is an oval, sloping up towards the right. This is easily made with a single stroke of the pen, a little additional pressure on completing the shape filling it in if necessary. The value of this shape, as opposed to a circle, is best seen in the writing of closely filled chords.

Open notes are now confined to the rare breve (larger values being virtually obsolete), semibreve, and minim. The simplest form of breve is a semibreve (a mere open note-head) bounded by two upright lines the depth of a stave space. Note-heads without stems need not be inclined.

The never-ending subdivisions of a crotchet are made by adding tails to the stem, either as a sharply angled line, or an imitation of the graceful curve used by the engraver.

The latter takes no longer to draw in practice and when used in quantity has a far less violent effect on the eye. The more tails required, the more elongated the stem must be. Tails are always written on the right-hand side of the stems except under certain conditions in beaming.

Stems are normally best about three stave lines deep, though this will have to be varied in cases of many tails, close part-writing, cueing, and grace-notes. Those in a downward direction are attached to the left of the note-head, those upward, to the right. Notes above the centre line of any stave have downward stems, those below have upward stems. A note on the centre line may have a stem up or down, the position of the surrounding notes determining what is most consistent; in cases of doubt, it should be turned down. The stems of grace notes are turned upwards without exception, and except in extreme cases of range, those of cue notes are also always turned upwards. The stem should be drawn with a separate stroke from, though joined to, the note-head; attempts to combine the two separate movements into one result in unevenness, and only a little practice is needed to ensure that an accurate joint is made automatically.

Beams

Stems of successive quavers and smaller values are often joined at the tips of the stem with a beam, a line of thicker quality than the stem itself (though this is automatically taken care of by the pen). The notes are first written as crotchets, the beam being added afterwards; it should not extend beyond the stems of the first and last notes of the group. An exactly horizontal beam, if drawn within the stave, should either hang or rest on a line; two or more beams so drawn will allow the space between the stave lines to show clearly.

Note values shorter than a semiquaver will require longer stems than usual, although, unless the notes beamed together are identical, or proceed equidistantly, the length of stem is likely to vary considerably. Except in the rarest of cases, the stem should not be shortened to less than a length equal to three spaces on the stave.

It is best from a reading point of view to beam together no more than a minim's worth of quavers at one time (or a dotted minim's worth in compound time). Smaller values should be kept to a crotchet's worth (or dotted crotchet) and in cases of demisemiquavers or less the half division of a crotchet is shown by a break in the third and any additional beam:

Beaming 'across the beat', thereby obscuring the natural divisions of a bar, does not assist reading, and is best avoided.

Sometimes beaming across both the beat and the bar line is used to show irregular rhythmic groupings. There is much dissent amongst musicians as to whether this is preferable to traditional grouping or not. A good example may be found in Michael Tippett's Second Symphony, pages 5 and 6, in the string parts; another way of dealing with the problem occurs in the third movement of the same work. Whatever one's feelings about the complexity of the result it is beyond doubt that any number of accents, slurs, etc., applied to the same notes grouped in traditional fashion could not bring about the same irregular rhythmic sound. Without such an intention as this, however, no form of notation should be allowed to obscure the natural units of a bar.

Since all stems of notes beamed together must turn in the same direction, the actual direction taken is that demanded by the majority of notes under the beam. If there is no majority, conform with the surrounding passages. Again, in cases of doubt they turn downwards. Stems of beamed groups of notes will of necessity be of varying lengths; generally speaking the direction of the beaming will follow that suggested by the outer notes of the group, but care should be taken to allow for notes outside the general contour of a group.

The practice of writing such a note on the other side of a beam is to be avoided; if it is absolutely necessary, the majority of stems may be turned in the wrong direction.

In such an instance, or any one containing many notes under one beam, it is best to write only the note-heads first, then stem and join the first and last of a group, allowing enough space for good length stems from the other heads to be drawn in last. In groups of more than eight or so notes under one beaming it is better to draw at least the first beam with a ruler.

Alternating short and long notes may be beamed together; if the first note is a short one the extra beam will be on the right hand side of a stem. In all other cases it will be on the left, except in the case of dotted long notes and shorter ones together making a single component; in this case the beam points towards the dot. The following groupings show most procedures :

Two or three grace notes together are beamed as semiquavers, more than this as demisemiquavers. Incomplete and broken beams may be used to show changes of dynamics or separate contrapuntal lines. There are many examples of this in the organ and violin works of J. S. Bach.

Chords

The same principles of stemming up or down apply to chords, the demands of the majority of notes being followed. Stems will of course be longer to accommodate all the notes but the final exposed section of stem is best kept a little shorter than that of a single note. Seconds are written in ascending order on alternate sides of the stem, but as many notes as possible must be kept on the correct side.

Chords may be written with either the top note first and a downward stem long enough to take the remaining notes, or the bottom note first with a similar upward stem. Alternatively, all the note-heads for the correct side of the stem may be written first, the stem and any displaced notes added afterwards. In this method it will be found quicker to work from the top downwards if the stem is to be turned down, or from the bottom upwards if it is to be turned up.

Part-Writing

If two parts are on one stave then all the tails of the upper part will turn up, and those of the lower, down. Shared pitches may share the same stem only in the case of extended unison passages; they may share the same note-head, with separate stems, only if the value is the same; otherwise two note-heads are also necessary, written as if they were crossing seconds. Simultaneous sounds are of course vertically aligned, but seconds (unless the parts cross) are written in the reverse order to their position in chords, to secure a better visual effect. The following example, though unlikely from a musical point of view, displays all the above principles.

Note the placing of accidentals and particularly the repetitions within the bar at *, where one of the voices has the note for the first time in the bar, and also the use of the natural in the second bar for the second voice, necessary to cancel the sharp already used for the first voice (unlikely to appear in good part-writing!). If the passage were intended for one performer the repetitions could be omitted, but not the cancellation.

Cues

Much will be said later about the functions of cues. They should be written as small notes, with much shorter stems, all of which are turned upwards except when the range is extreme. The rests for the main instrument are normally placed lower than usual on the stave, but depending on the position of the cue-notes they might need to be higher, or out of the stave altogether. Leger lines for cues are kept the normal distance from the stave and each other, and not correspondingly contracted.

CHAPTER THREE

Accessory Symbols

Arpeggios

The normal wavy arpeggio sign before a chord indicates an upward roll; if a downward roll is required an arrow is added to the foot of the line. If upward and downward rolls are used in combination, it is best to add the arrow to the top of the sign for the upward roll also. In two-stave parts the sign must be carried through from top to bottom, unless a roll beginning simultaneously in each hand is required.

Harp chords are almost invariably rolled slightly. If this effect is not required the instruction 'non arpegg.' should be added. In string music all chords of three or more notes are slightly arpeggiated. Extra bow pressure can reduce this to a minimum; a bracket placed before the chord will indicate this, though such a sign also signifies 'non divisi' in orchestral passages; the written instruction 'non arpegg.' can also be used.

Arpeggio signs are placed before a chord, never after.

Bar Lines

These should extend from the top to the bottom of the stave exactly. In two-stave parts they will be drawn as one single line through both staves and the space between them, and in scores they are best carried completely through each separate choir of instruments. A bar line occupies about three quarters of the space horizontally required by a note, though it has no duration in time, of course. A double bar line is used for added significance, to draw attention to a new section, a key change, or the end of a piece. Such final lines look best if the second is thicker than the first.

There is a tendency amongst some composers to dispense with the double bar altogether, except for the end of a piece. However, the visual effect of subdividing a longer work with an appropriate double bar will often maintain the interest of the performer.

Time permitting, I would seriously recommend that all bar lines should be ruled, even those through single staves. They can be drawn lightly as the music is written, and inked over using a ruler, and preferably the narrower nib when the page is dry, or better still when the part is finished. Not only is the appearance remarkably improved by the slightly thicker, accurately upright lines, but this 'going-over' of the work often reveals an error one may have forgotten to correct, or didn't even know had been made. The time taken is little, three staves can be dealt with at once, and the result is well worth it.

The bar divided between two lines sometimes cannot be avoided; for example, a passage of bars each containing thirty-two demisemiquavers in $\frac{4}{4}$ time, plus accidentals, will look cramped if two bars are fitted on to a line, and too spread to convey the speed of the notes if written one bar to a line. Unless the bar can be divided exactly into two, however, it should not be split between lines. When it is necessary, a small inclined 'equals' sign should be placed at the end of the stave (not a dotted bar line), and any accidentals arising in the first half of the bar must be repeated on the new line.

The dotted bar line should be avoided if possible, though it may be used to show an unusual division of a normally regular bar, or a change of tempo taking place during a bar.

Brackets and Braces; Systems

All the staves of a score are connected at the extreme left by a single unadorned line to form a system—a group of staves forming one line of music. A bracket is then added to join the staves of separate choirs (i.e. woodwind, brass, strings, etc.). A second bracket is further added to join staves of like instruments (e.g., Clarinets 1 and 2 if they are written on different staves, Violins 1 and 2, etc.). In chamber music for like instruments (e.g. woodwind quartet) the first bracket will embrace all staves. Single-stave parts are left open.

The second bracket is often replaced by the decorative brace used to connect the staves of piano and similar music. This is a difficult sign to make freehand, however, and a neater effect will be obtained using a bracket in all instances. A comparison of the first pages of standard printings of a classic for large orchestra will reveal these features and their variants.

Harmonics

Harmonic signs have different meanings in string music, woodwind music, and harp music. (The method of note production on brass instruments renders them inappropriate.)

Harmonics on stringed instruments are produced in two ways (and unfortunately written in many more): natural harmonics by lightly stopping the open string, false harmonics by the full stopping of the string—thus making a new length—plus a further light stopping. Despite the variations frequently seen, they should both be notated in the same way. The open string or the fully stopped note is written in the usual way as an ordinary note; to the stem is also added an open diamond-shaped note showing the lighter stopping to produce the harmonic. This shape is not difficult to draw with practice, and it should never be filled in, as in handwritten music it becomes almost indistinguishable from an ordinary note, and can easily be misread as an ordinary double stopping.

The practice of adding the note actually produced as in the first example above is not necessary; no other note can properly result from what is already written, and it can become confusing in a long passage of harmonics. The first two harmonics above are natural, the second two false; the practice of omitting the open string note when writing natural harmonics should not be followed, since the relative values of each can only be shown by writing a filled-in diamond in the first case. No violinist would attempt to play either as a false harmonic on the G string. An exception to this rule is the natural octave harmonic, which is written using the actual note sounded with a small 'o' above.

This method is also used in the higher positions where the natural harmonic is the same sound as the note actually stopped.

The use of 'o' should be restricted to these instances only. The same symbol is also used to denote an open string, but since all the open strings and their natural octave harmonics have no common sounding note, confusion will not arise.

Other methods of notating harmonics are often met with, but none can be said to improve on the foregoing. The practice of not using ties for diamond-shaped notes when appropriate seems particularly misleading.

Guitar harmonics, however, are best written with diamond-shaped notes only, showing the point of touch: this enables chords to be clearly notated. To avoid confusion between crotchets and minims the former must be written with filled-in diamonds; extra care is then needed to preserve the angled shape.

Woodwind harmonics are written with the symbol 'o' above the actual note to be sounded. Since all notes above the first octave or twelfth are harmonics anyway, this is understood to be an instruction to produce the note by means of a false fingering (giving in effect a 'false' harmonic); the quality of the sound is affected, not necessarily adversely.

Harp harmonics are written in the same manner as woodwind harmonics, that is, with an 'o' above the note, but the sound produced is an octave higher. This is the only practical harp harmonic, and it has no effect in the highest register.

The practice of also writing the actual note sounded is not necessary; writing only the resulting sound with the 'o', requires the addition of the words 'sounds as written' and is therefore rather pointless.

Harmonics are possible though rare on other instruments; for example they may be obtained by stopping the strings inside the piano. But any composer resorting to these should include in his score instructions on their production, since none can be said to be common practice as yet.

It should be noted that the symbol 'o' is always written above the note, never below. Used in brass music, the symbol denotes a return to 'open' or normal note production after muting or stopping (+).

Irregular Note Values

Any division of a unit into irregular components requires the addition of a number showing such a division. The most common example is the introduction of a triplet into simple time.

Note the addition of a bracket (not a rounded slur) for groups not beamed together. The principle guiding the value of these notes is that they are played more quickly than if the number were not there; the number has the effect of reducing the value of the note. The number and bracket should be applied to the stem end of the notes whenever possible, though reasons of clarity might require it to be placed over the heads (in this instance a bracket is used with beamed notes also). The bracket should embrace the outer stems, not close between them.

A regular succession of such groups requires no more than one figure for the first and the abbreviation 'sim.' (simile) under the second.

Confusion often arises in compound time and in irregular metres. It will not do so if the principle of 'reducing value' is always used; but an explanation of the alternative is necessary, even though it should be rejected as a method. Accurate notation of simple irregularities in compound time can be achieved by use of the time dot. Thus in the following example the accurate notation in the first bar is sometimes written as in the second with numbers instead of dots. Sometimes both numbers and dots are used together, but this would be quite meaningless if logically translated.

It will be seen that here the number increases the value of the notes. This method may be extended to include more complex irregularities, such as groups of fives and sevens, giving rise to the following:

It is not easy to recognize this immediately as a $\frac{12}{8}$ bar at all. Using the reducing-value method always employed in simple time the previous two examples would read:

I find this immediately clear and much to be preferred.

Sometimes a ratio is used instead of a single number; this is not normally necessary, but helpful in the first example following, and essential in the second, where a division of the irregular bar could not be deduced without it.

Note that in the last bar, the first group is played slower than the second; if all the notes were to be equal, they would all be beamed together and the figure 14 added.

The ratio marking can then be seen to be essential when a group can be reduced to more than one regular group containing the same note values (e.g. seven in the time of six or four, thirteen in the time of twelve or eight etc.). It should not be used with the smaller figure first (i.e. 2:3) since this will merely show that the wrong notation has been used.

Finally it should be remembered that two regular triplets do not make a regular sextuplet; the rhythmic implications of each are different.

Leger Lines

Leger lines, being natural extensions of the stave, should in theory be placed exactly the same distance apart as the stave lines. In practice it is likely to be found that the line drawn by the pen is a little thicker than the printed line, and consequently the leger lines might have to be very slightly wider apart to accommodate the same symbols. It should not be necessary to point out that they should remain constantly equidistant whether filled with notes or not; the days should have surely passed when the following horror might appear on the music stand before some unfortunate player.

Except in the case of chords all the lines for a note should be drawn first; it will be easier to build the chord upwards by notes and lines as appropriate; accidentals are best added after the note or chord has been written.

Passages on leger lines, it will be noted, occupy far more lateral space than identical ones between the staves. This is because in addition to the normal space between note-heads there is an amount of leger line protruding from each side of the note-head; this should be kept to the absolute minimum necessary to make it obvious. For this reason leger lines for smaller notes, such as cues or grace notes, will be shorter than those for regular notes, though they must still remain equidistant from each other and the stave lines.

Octave Signs

To avoid the excessive use of leger lines the octave sign '8va' may be used. In scores it may be used freely, but in orchestral and other parts its use should be restricted to keyboard instruments as far as possible. '8va' should be written over the first note to which it applies, or just preceding it if there is a rest; a dotted line is carried over all the relevant notes, and a downward stroke used to close the instruction. The addition of the word 'loco' to the first note returning to normal is optional. Care should be taken that the dotted line does not interfere with any other markings to the notes (slurs in particular are liable to suffer); it should in fact be drawn above everything except tempo directions.

The same sign may be applied to notes in the bass clef to be played an octave lower, being written beneath everything (except a piano pedalling mark) and the dotted line closed with an upward stroke; the addition of the word 'bassa' to the '8va' is not necessary. A displacement of two octaves may be noted using '15ma' (not '16va'), but this is rarely truly necessary.

An octave sign placed under or over a passage applies to all the notes on that stave, but those only. Thus in keyboard music if the notes on both staves are to be played an octave higher, a sign is necessary for each stave. In rare cases, such as a widely spread cluster, it may be applied to a group of notes only on a stave, the others being marked 'loco'.

Because it destroys the visual contour of phrases when used for a few notes only, the sign is best employed for a reasonable length at a time.

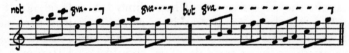

Ornaments and Trills

Ornaments are now generally written out in full, but any sign used follows the printer's version, and is placed above the note, except for a lower part sharing a stave. Trills can be notated in many ways; by far the best is to include the auxiliary note in brackets. This will take care of trilling with any interval either above or below the main note. The inclusion of the wavy line is recommended, even for single short notes, carried to the point at which the trill ends.

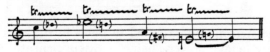

If a trill is to continue through two or more notes they should be tied together; if the trill is to begin again a new sign

is necessary. Double trills require a sign each; except in parts
sharing a stave the sign is placed over the stave.

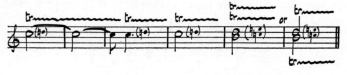

Slurs and Ties

Slurs begin and end at the centre of a note-head, or if necessary
the tip of a stem, but they do not touch either. The curve
should be kept as flat as possible, to keep the slur close to the
notes. Slurs should always run from note-head to note-head
when possible.

The position of the last slur would be permissible for space
reasons.

Ties curve either from note-head to note-head or, better,
from and to the sides of the heads; in the case of chords or in
confined spaces the latter is the only course available. Used in
conjunction with slurs the ties are written 'inside' (i.e., closer
to the notes than the slur). The curve of a tie, which should be
very flat indeed, follows the opposite direction to the stems of
the tied notes (or in the case of unstemmed notes, the direction
they would take). In chords the outer ties take opposite
directions; ties for seconds also take opposite directions except
when they appear as clusters.

In combinations of slurs and ties it is advisable to replace as many tied notes as possible with longer values to avoid a confusion of curves. The first version here is to be preferred.

Staccato dots, tenuto marks, and accents are placed beneath slurs; generally speaking, the slur embraces all other markings, though in some instances expression marks will have to appear simultaneously above and below a note.

Tempo and Dynamic Markings

All tempo indications and metronome marks are placed above the stave, and above all other symbols (except rehearsal figures); this rule is invariable under any circumstance. Written tempo directions, and for that matter all other verbal directions, should be written in lower case (except for necessary capitals) disconnected letters, as in printing, and not joined as in normal cursive handwriting.

All dynamic markings are placed beneath the stave, or between the staves for two-stave instruments. This rule is variable for independent parts sharing a stave, and in vocal music, where all dynamics are placed above to avoid confusion with the text. Marks of accentuation, marcato, spiccato, staccato, tenuto, etc., should be applied to the note-head, unless space makes it absolutely impossible; this situation can usually be avoided. Crescendo markings and their opposites should begin and end exactly at the appropriate points and not be allowed to wander uncertainly.

Most of the symbols used by the printer are easily copied;

the spiccato or wedge-staccato is quickly drawn as a down and up stroke in the shape of a V, making the angle so acute that the ink on both sides of the stroke runs together.

Time Dots

Time dots are always placed in a space, alongside the note if it too occupies a space, or in the space above (though still to the right) if the note is on a line. (In rare instances, further adjustment is needed.) If the note is further tied, the tie begins from the note, though in handwritten music it is often clearer if the tie begins after the dot.

Further dots may be added, but more than two are rare. Each further dot adds half the value added by the previous one. The effect is additional, not multiple; note particularly that ♩‥ equals only ♩+♪+♪ and does not fill a ⁹⁄₈ bar (♩.+♩.). A dot may no longer be used to extend the value of a note beyond a bar line, though this device may still be seen in modern printed scores of Brahms's orchestral works.

CHAPTER FOUR

Spacing and Alignment

The horizontal spacing and vertical alignment of notes and rests on a page of music is of the utmost importance. That music should be written on the page in a manner giving rise to ease of reading, clarity of intention, and general tidiness will be obvious. Anyone writing a page of music should bear in mind that in all probability it is for somebody else to read. For it to be immediately understandable a few further simple principles need to be observed. Not even the most attractive hand is of much use if the notes it writes are placed just anywhere on the page.

Horizontal Spacing

Except in very rare cases or by mere coincidence, the physical length of a bar of music is not precisely relative to its musical length (each two centimetres of music on a page will probably not have the same duration). Nevertheless, all other things being equal, notes of the same value should be evenly spaced on the page and combinations of uneven values spaced with regard to their respective values. Thus minims should be spaced further apart than crotchets, semiquavers closer than quavers, and so on. An exact proportion would, of course, be ridiculous; a minim will not require the same space as eight semiquavers. The distances will be decided by the content of the music itself; a passage dominated by crotchets will not

have them all widely spaced to accommodate a few semiquavers, any more than a passage full of quavers will be all
cramped together the better to display a solitary minim. The
undesirable disregard of the relationship between duration and
space can be seen from the following; compare it with the
second version, which is much more acceptable to the eye.

This regard for proper spacing will soon become second nature
after much practical work at writing.

The planning of a single line of music is governed by this
placing; it will not do to rule bar lines of equal length in
advance and hope to be able to fit in the music. The number
of bars to a line will vary considerably, but it does not take
much experience to become aware of what is possible. In my
own case, I very soon discovered that three $\frac{4}{4}$ bars of Handelian
semiquavers were all I could fit legibly on one line; whereas
the same line could just as legibly take seven bars of
Monteverdian minims or even eleven of Byrd's breves (not, it
will be noticed, the same number of notes in any case).

Accidentals, it should be remembered, require as much
space as a note-head, and a generous helping of these added
to the Handel example might well reduce it to two bars per
line.

Vertical Alignment

Except, again, in rare instances, the notes placed under one
another in a score or a part (i.e., vertically aligned) are to be
sounded together. This may seem too obvious to mention, but

a look through many scores written by comparatively inexperienced hands will make it seem an exception rather than a rule. Vertical alignment is the most difficult thing the writer of music must learn to deal with, for unless he takes the totally impractical step of writing his score in a downward direction, like Chinese, he must proceed by a trial and error method, making allowances in each line he writes for what is to happen below; a large score, in fact, is best tackled bar by bar, with the most active line written first. In due course, enough experience will be gained to enable one to plan far in advance and to write one part at a time for one or maybe more pages. Even the most experienced writer, however, occasionally has to begin a page anew, owing to a miscalculation or an oversight.

All the principles of horizontal spacing apply in dealing with vertical alignment. If all the various parts of a score moved in exactly the same rhythm (of which a simple example is a passage of double octaves in a piano score) there would be no further problem. It is more likely, however, that where one part has a minim, another might have crotchets, and another quavers; the horizontal spacing of the various components of any bar will therefore differ to allow for these occurrences. Any line of a score viewed individually might consequently seem badly spaced; the experienced hand which automatically writes good horizontally spaced parts needs to be continually 'corrected' by the mind which stores all the forthcoming pitfalls brought about by vertical alignment.

All notes placed under each other begin to sound at the same moment; rests also are placed at the beginning of the silence (except for full bar rests, which are placed centrally). Allowance must therefore also be made for the inserting of an accidental in one part, or the change of a clef, still further affecting the horizontal aspect. The following example will show a number of such displacements after an initial bar of purely horizontal considerations.

Note that in all chords, including those with seconds and clusters, it is the notes on the 'correct' side of the stem which are aligned. Crossing parts are also aligned by note-head, with a very small adjustment to keep the stemming clear; except for seconds, which are written in ascending order, as

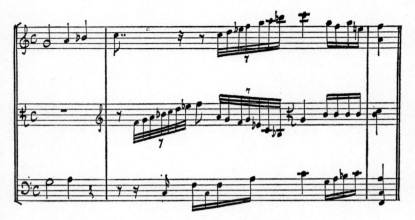

already stated on p. 27 (ordinary non-crossing seconds are written in reverse order). Dotted bar lines in uneven measures added merely as an aid to vertical alignment are of no value if the work is properly aligned to begin with; if it isn't, they serve only to draw attention to the fact.

Still further problems of alignment arise in writing vocal music: these will be dealt with later.

There is no other way to conquer the problems posed in vertical aligning than by experience. It will take some time to be able to bear in mind all the necessary adjustments to the natural horizontal spacing at once. It is also one aspect of music writing that can never become second nature.

Part II: Practice

CHAPTER FIVE

Some First Attempts

The first article I ever read on the subject of actually writing down music was in a popular musical journal, and written by an arranger whose name commanded enough respect for his article to be taken seriously. Almost incredibly, it began with something like these words: 'Take the pen, dip it into the ink bottle, and write your first two or three notes of music.' I recommend anybody inexperienced in writing down music to do just that, before considering his next sentences. 'Was there too much ink on the pen? Very likely, or, if you were guarding against that, probably too little.'

The point was made; the first essential of a good, neat appearance in writing is a uniform flow of ink throughout a page of work. A mixture of thick notes and thin, standing out and near-invisible, is very trying to the eye, looks untidy, reproduces disastrously, and is quite unnecessary. In these days of ball-point pens, felt-tips, nylon-tips, and other pre-inked instruments, the art of combining separate pen and ink may need a little practice. But experience will soon teach one how to regulate the amount of ink flowing on to the paper.

Experience is, of course, the answer to many problems. Not long ago I was asked by a student how to avoid another unfortunate visual effect, the stave line of music on which the bars are so spaced as to leave a blank section of stave at the right-hand end. I was reminded of the famous conductor, asked by a student how to get the orchestra in exactly at the end of the soloist's scale passage in the last movement of Beethoven's Fourth Piano Concerto, who disarmingly replied

'It is all a matter of luck!' What he meant, of course, was that there was no 'rule' and only experience would solve the problem. So it is with fitting a number of bars exactly on to a given length of stave. Plan ahead in all cases, and eventually sufficient experience will be acquired for it to happen correctly without even thinking about it.

I recently cleared out the attic of my house; no hidden masterpieces came to light, but I did discover some old manuscripts of pieces written during my first year at music college. I was very interested to look through these to discover what notational problems I had as a student. My manuscript was always praised during my time at college; looking at it now I can only observe that this said very little for the quality of that of my fellow students. Obviously, I had little knowledge of the rules set out in the preceding chapters, and it would certainly have been to my ultimate advantage had a few weeks been devoted to learning these before beginning to write pieces in the style of whoever we had been discussing, or incorporating some harmonic or technical features. But strangely we never were taught any of the fundamentals of notation at college, and as far as I am aware this area of musical education is still largely ignored.

Most of us in our student days are determined to 'shake the world' in some way or another, and it seems that I had intended to include changing the system of notation amongst my contributions to the progress of music. Fortunately, in the course of time all or most of us conform to the accepted traditions, developing them if need be, rather than casting them aside in favour of pointless novelty. Certainly no innovation which is not an improvement is worth consideration. It is not very likely that any student is going to discover in a flash a much improved way of notating something; our present system has evolved over a number of years, and sooner or—regrettably—later most of us are going to accept the tried and proven methods of notation, provided that our musical ideas can be expressed by them. It may well be that we are not initially ready to conform simply because we are not aware of the rules.

One of these early pieces of mine demonstrates quite forcibly the need to present one's ideas to the performer in the most straightforward manner. Our class had been discussing the use of remote keys, and had been set an exercise in C sharp major; my piece, not unnaturally, modulated to A sharp minor and then into the major. Of course, I was unable to resist using a key signature of ten sharps. As I presented my manuscript for its customary play-through, my professor vacated the piano stool, saying 'Very interesting; play it for me.' Needless to say, I was soon in quite unnecessary difficulties, none of which would have existed with a key signature of two flats.

In this connection I have on my desk at the moment a symphony by a not unknown composer, written in the key of C sharp minor, which shows throughout the composer's reluctance to write enharmonically. Thus there are passages in the keys of E sharp major, and also F flat major; difficult enough for instruments playing a single line but, I suspect, near impossible for the many keyboard players required to play extremely chromatic rapid sequences of chords in either of these remote keys. The number of missing accidentals in this particular score also demonstrates the composer's unfamiliarity with these keys. At one point there is even a passage in B sharp major; I wonder what the composer thought had been gained by asking a pianist to play the passage at (a) below, instead of the enharmonic (b).

Perhaps the most obvious fault of my own writing in those early days was a continual slant from bottom left to top right. I can offer two reasons for this appearance, which still invades my work to some extent if not constantly guarded against. It is not simple to make a stroke quickly and exactly at right angles to a given line, and this difficulty increases if one does not sit immediately in line with the work page. Very often I find the page that I am working on is some distance to the right of centre, particularly if I am copying from another page on the left. Furthermore, I have a distant recollection of being taught to adopt this particular slant when first learning cursive handwriting. A constant guard against this tendency, and the use of a backing sheet (when appropriate), as recommended earlier, should go a long way towards rectifying this fault.

Next I notice that my note-heads are far too small. I do still write very small note-heads when sketching arrangements or composing—so small, in fact, that they are almost indistinguishable from the stems. This work, however, is for me alone; I can read it, and make a respectable copy from it, even if nobody else can. I must say that I find the very smallest of rounded heads easier to read than the method used by some composers of writing a horizontal dash for a note-head in a space, and an inclined dash for one on a line. The reader can decide for himself from the following example.

Smallish note-heads in themselves are perhaps not such a bad fault; obviously I had no trouble in writing a six-white-note cluster with all the heads on one side of the stem—as it happens, on the wrong side of the stem, as explained in the next paragraph. Unfortunately, the other components of the page become adversely affected, as the horizontal spacing is reduced accordingly, giving a very cramped appearance. Particularly in writing piano and other keyboard music a definite relationship between horizontal and vertical spacing is demanded, and this is basically governed by the distance between the two staves. The further apart the staves are, the greater the space must be between horizontal events. This can easily be seen by writing the same keyboard passage on a page of ten-stave paper and then again on a page of twenty-four staves; comparison of the two will demonstrate the necessary relationships between notes and spaces. Much of the cramped appearance of my writing in those days was also apparently due to using a pen with too fine a nib: the few strokes necessary to form a note actually produced a far smaller one than that recommended earlier.

The most obvious fault of all is an 'innovation'—not necessarily of my own invention, as I subsequently discovered it actually recommended in an otherwise admirable if out-of-date text book. That was to write virtually all the note-heads to the left of the stem, regardless of the direction of the latter. My opinion of this sort of innovation has frequently been mentioned before. Fortunately, I was cured of this and other idiosyncrasies before long; had I known the rules in advance, I might never have strayed in the first place.

The rules set out in the preceding chapters cannot be deduced merely from looking at a printed page; we only sense the existence of a rule when we notice something wrong. Had I had knowledge of the rules in advance I would have begun notating my first pieces with a background of fact, rather than using what I thought I had seen on the printed page as a guide. The following chapters will suggest how these rules may be applied to specific areas of music. However obvious some of it might seem, there will, I think, always be somebody who has not previously realized how or why something is done in a particular way.

As a last thought, before consigning my youthful indiscretions to the flames, I would observe that those in pencil have almost faded away, those written with a ball-point pen have off-set on to the opposite page, resulting in an almost illegible mess, whilst those written in normal ink have lasted perhaps better than they deserved!

CHAPTER SIX

Keyboard Music

Simple Piano Music

Perhaps the first and simplest type of piano music the student is required to write down is the straightforward harmonization of melody. This should present no problems, the melody being written in the upper stave (right hand) and simple chords, probably only on the beat, in the lower stave (left hand). It is better to write vertical events as they occur, rather than writing eight bars of melody first, for example, and then returning to fill in the chords. It will soon be found that a succession of chords requires more space horizontally than the same number of single notes. In the unlikely event of the harmonization needing to be written in the treble clef, a change of clef in the lower stave is preferable to writing the left-hand part in the upper stave.

As far as possible the separate staves should be reserved for separate hands, but obviously the more complex the music becomes the more difficult this will be. In the event of either hand passing into the 'other' stave, all stems for right-hand music go up and all those for left-hand go down, irrespective of the position of the notes on the stave. The same is true of chords divided between the staves. No rests are necessary in the portion of a stave left empty in such cases, but independent rests are needed for each hand even when they share a stave.

Polyphonic Music

A more sophisticated type of harmony, that in a very definite four parts (almost invariably distributed two to each hand) can be laid out in several ways. Separate stemming of each part is not really necessary unless the note values of parts on the same stave differ. On the other hand, if the values are constantly changing (and we are now approaching counter-point rather than harmony), the result might be clearer if the voices are always separated.

The more contrapuntally complex the music becomes, the more difficult it is to show the progress of each voice clearly. The composer should always bear in mind how many voices the pianist's fingers can be expected to display clearly (the five-part fugues in Bach's 48 Preludes and Fugues are about the reasonable limit); but fortunately most piano chording using many notes is just vertical harmony and not independent many-voiced counterpoint.

A large number of independent parts can be shown on one stave, however, if necessary, using a little careful displacement.

Such a passage, if really intended for one (left) hand might be better displayed on two staves, with another (or even two more) used for the right hand. The most famous example of four-stave writing is probably that in Rachmaninoff's C sharp minor Prelude, though it has always seemed to me that this particular section could be laid out equally clearly on two staves. Obviously, it is easier to take in the contents of two staves at a glance than four.

An extremely complex combining of parts on to one stave can be found in the central section of Chopin's F sharp major Nocturne, where the right hand alone combines melody, two counter-patterns, and an accompaniment (in addition to the left hand's independent accompaniment). Spreading this on to two staves would not help in clarifying this passage since most of the notes serve two functions at the same time; neither did the version I once came across, written in F major and $\frac{4}{4}$ time with the note-values doubled, and only the melody and accompaniment marked in the right hand.

Special Problems

Problems of notation peculiar to the piano and other keyboard instruments almost all arise from its use of more than one stave, and the need to show clearly the flow of music throughout these staves. (The remaining problems nearly all develop from the ease with which two or more notes can be played simultaneously.) The very existence of two staves has tempted composers to use certain devices, very few of which seem to be improvements on traditional methods. Thus time signatures may be seen written between the staves instead of in them; the resulting break in the flow of music can be quite disconcerting.

I have also seen rests used in this fashion, but in a case like the following it seems far better to give the necessary rest to the hand first playing.

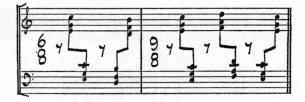

Simultaneous groups of notes in both staves are sometimes seen joined by a central beam, but in no instance can this be said to be an improvement on the more usual method.

The occasional use of this method to join single events, as in the last crotchet above, has a most unsettling look.

Arpeggios, on the other hand, often pass through both staves, when a common beam is essential.

Chords broken between the hands can be treated in the same manner. (Avoid the temptation to fill the gaps with unnecessary rests.)

Chords for one hand sometimes straddle the staves; because of the position of the stem lines in the following example (a) would be for the right hand and (b) for the left; the strange-looking (c) sometimes encountered could presumably be for either or both. Because of the limited stretch of the hand, however, there is rarely an instance where a version of (d) or (e) could not be better substituted.

If ties are involved with chords for both hands on the one stave, all ties for right hand-notes have an upward curve, and those for left hand-notes a downward one.

It is possible to tie from one stave (or hand) to the other, though this is an aspect of notation which never looks totally happy in either of its two versions.

Although (a) is perhaps the most logical, (b) releases a greater amount of space between the staves which might well be needed

59

for other things (slurs, dynamics, etc.). I have seen (b) written with the addition at bar two of 'take over from left hand', but this would seem too obvious to merit inclusion.

Slurs can easily be over-used in piano music. In the simplest of cases, such as melody with harmony, one slur above the system is normally sufficient, and nothing further will be conveyed by adding another beneath the system. If different slurring is required for each hand the normal procedure is for right-hand slurring to be placed over the respective stave and left-hand slurring under the stave. There are, however, so many likely variations that almost every case needs individual consideration. As always, the aim should be to make the intention as clear as possible; the rule of slurring from note-head to note-head, as in single-line parts, is generally suspended.

Slurs which cross from one stave to the other must be placed in such a position as to leave the maximum amount of space between the staves for other markings.

Pedals

Pedal markings in the simpler types of music are best omitted. To a considerable extent use of the pedal must be regarded as a prerogative of the performer; one should no more consider trying to notate every nuance of the pedal than prescribing the exact amount of vibrato for each note of a violin solo. A direction 'con ped.' is often sufficient. On the occasions it is necessary to include pedal markings these are placed beneath the lower stave.

For the damper pedal, also called the sustaining pedal, though this name can give rise to confusion (and also quite erroneously called the 'loud pedal'), the standard marking of 'Ped.' at the point of depression and an asterisk at the point of release is sufficient. The additional drawing of a line during the period of depression will do nothing more than confuse. The half release, if required, can be shown by an inverted V at the exact point with a short horizontal line drawn either side.

The soft pedal is marked by the term 'una corda', with 'tre corde' at the point of release. If used at the same moment as other pedals this marking can be placed between the staves, like a dynamic marking, in the interests of clarity.

The third pedal found on concert grands is the sostenuto pedal (which is a sound reason for calling the damper pedal by this latter name only). This pedal will sustain only those notes whose keys are depressed at the moment of pedal depression (though certain tricky modifications are possible), and is particularly useful in sustaining an organ pedal type bass, whilst enabling both hands to articulate florid upper passages clearly. It is best marked 'S.P.' or 'P.3' at the point of depression. The duration of the depression is often marked by a slanting line ending in a downward stroke for release, but the longer the duration the more complex this becomes, and if lines are also drawn for the damper pedal the results can be unintelligible. A small right-angle surmounted by an arrow (see example below) for the point of release is quite clear; I don't think there can be any doubt of the intentions in the following passage, however musically unlikely.

Probably the most commendable pedal marking of all—at least for the amateur pianist—is 'senza ped.'.

Dynamics

Dynamic markings are usually intended for both hands, certainly so in our simpler efforts. They are placed centrally between the staves; in the event of this position becoming overfull, they can be placed above or even below the system. Care must then be taken to ensure that whilst they are close enough not to be overlooked, they are not so close as to be mistaken for dynamics for one hand only. This is exceptional, however; dynamics should and nearly always will fit between the staves. Those intended for one hand or even one part only should obviously be placed as close to the affected part as possible.

The layout on the page of keyboard music will depend on its content, but unless it is of the simplest nature and well contained within the staves, or an orchestral part consisting mainly of rests, the inclusion of a blank stave between the systems will greatly add to the clarity. No well-printed page of piano music has the same space between systems as between staves forming a system. It is possible to obtain paper specially ruled for keyboard writing, which takes this into account; I think it is a matter of personal taste whether this is used or not.

Clusters and Harmonics

Keyboard clusters are notated in many different ways; the one to be recommended is that which joins the centre of the note-heads at the extremities of the cluster by a thick black line; alternatively an incomplete stem on the wrong side of the note-head may be used, though two such stems are necessary for normally unstemmed notes.

As written here the cluster would be played on the white keys; the addition of a flat to the outer note-heads (or even centrally, though less effectively here) would indicate a cluster on the black keys; the use of the sharp in this context is superfluous. Such notation over small intervals such as a fifth is easily misread in manuscript, and it is better to write out the notes required in such instances, as it also is with a one-handed chromatic cluster. This, and a safe way of avoiding ambiguity in other cases, can be seen in the piano part of Roberto Gerhard's *Epithalamion*.

Piano harmonics, most practical at the octave, produced by silently depressing one key and striking another, usually in conjunction with the pedal, are written in the normal way, but with diamond-shaped notes for the 'silent' keys. Any more elaborate trickery is best explained verbally in both score and part.

Other Keyboard Instruments

Organ music is usually written on three staves, the upper two for manuals, the lower for pedals only, though the pedal part may often be incorporated in the lower manual stave, provided it remains absolutely clear. Bar lines join the manual staves but the pedal stave is barred separately. Registration, where given, is written above the stave to which it refers; the symbols ∪ and ∧ (and their variants) for heel and toe are placed above the pedal stave for the right foot and below for the left.

Pedals on the harpsichord are a means of changing registration, and such markings as a change from 8ft. to 4ft. sounds are written between or above the staves like organ registration.

(See also p. 112.)

CHAPTER SEVEN
Vocal Music

General Principles

In vocal music both horizontal spacing and vertical alignment
are further affected by the addition of words. Words composed
of many letters often last no longer than shorter ones, and an
allowance must be made for this when including a text in
music writing. Each syllable of a word is placed under the
note to which it is to be sung, the division of words, if necessary,
following the practice found in any standard dictionary. As
a rough guide, however, a syllable generally begins with a
consonant, not a vowel (e.g. di-vi-sion). Word placing will
adversely affect the horizontal spacing of notes; anyone
doubting this should write the seven words 'fought, though
strength drained out, and died' to any passage of four semiquavers followed by three minims, and study the result.

There are in practice various methods of notating vocal
music, particularly with regard to the beaming and separate
tailing of groups of notes. I would most strongly advise
against any departure from the normal practice with non-
vocal music. Giving separate tails to single notes, and beaming
together groups of notes for single syllables, has two distinct
disadvantages.

Through sounds of mu- sic, strength was__ found and came a- new.__

First, the grouping of the notes often totally destroys the immediate visual identification of the units and natural rhythm of the bar, even when they are not as irregular as above; secondly, even if this fault could be accepted, the placing of the words, as already explained, destroys the natural horizontal spacing of the notes; an occasional flourish in an accompaniment, were it included, might affect this still further. The result resembles a drunken plainchant.

Normal beaming of notes, using slurs to show extended syllables, is a far more satisfying solution, and goes at least some way towards restoring the balance. If the text is properly underlaid, the slur may be dispensed with, particularly if a non-legato style of singing is required.

Note the position of the hyphen in 'mu-sic', widely spaced, and that a line is drawn from the 'type-line' of the word 'was' to show its extension through three notes. The same principle is applied to 'anew' involving a tied note, the punctuation—here a full stop—being inserted first.

In passages involving many short notes of unequal values it will sometimes be found necessary totally to suspend all horizontal spacing rules; if the words so demand, it can be necessary to give more space to a short note than a longer one (see the experiment referred to in the opening paragraph of this chapter). Sanity should be restored as soon as possible, however, and it is perhaps best to regard such instances as individual and temporary expansions.

The letters of any written text, like other written words in music, should be separated, and not joined as in normal handwriting. Since the text, with one or two rare exceptions, is placed beneath the notes, all other indications of dynamics and style which are not actually applied to a note-head are placed above the stave, so that the text may remain entirely clear. A text should not be written entirely in capital letters; these are more difficult to read in groups than lower-case letters.

The breath, where it is thought necessary to indicate it, is shown either by a comma or a V with an elongated right arm, like a tick. Placing it in brackets signifies 'take it if you need it' and this is an arrangement best left to the choirmaster.

Hymns and Chants

The simplest types of vocal writing (other than a single-line melody) are probably to be found in the hymn tune and psalm chant. These, if in the usual four parts, should be written on two staves, soprano and alto on one, tenor and bass on the other. Although the parts will most likely move together, I favour separate stemming of each voice when the music is intended to be read by singers.

Tradition has it that minims are used rather than crotchets, but this is a rule which has no real significance and may be adopted or rejected at will; shorter notes than the very occasional quaver, however, should be avoided.

The text can be added between the staves if there is room; in the simplest of cases, a blank stave can be left between the two staves of music for this purpose. Alternatively it can be added below; if many verses are involved this will be essential.

A psalm text will almost certainly be added below the music, since the pointing of the text will not allow it to be clearly written between the staves. Any standard hymn book or psalter will display these features.

Anthems and Part-Songs

The four-part anthem or part-song will need to be written on four staves, one for each voice. The text is now usually written twice, once between soprano and alto staves and once between tenor and bass, though if there are any significant differences between these groups of parts each will need its own separate line of text. In my experience, however, no singer is totally happy having to read a text from above a line of music (as happens to altos and basses in the above instance), and it is really preferable for the text to appear beneath every line of music.

When the tenor line is separated from the bass the voice is treated as a transposing one, and written in the treble clef, an octave higher than actually required. (This form of notation suits the natural tessitura of the voice.) A normal treble clef is sufficient, none of the other versions shown below adding anything significant, though (b) is sometimes useful to the eye, particularly in a large ensemble.

Simple divisions of the voices on one part can be incorporated in one stave, ideally with separate stemming; but in a work specifically requiring Sopranos 1 & 2, for example, each will need a separate stave. As the number of separate voices increases (the previous remarks hold good for all types of part-song, from two to forty parts and beyond) the task of writing text and dynamic instructions for each part becomes more and more laborious. There is no way of avoiding writing the text many times (and still producing a copy usable by all singers), but directions such as dynamics, if truly identical in every part, can be written in a large hand both above and below the system. This procedure, however, does become less adequate as the number of voices increases. When including directions above the actual vocal lines it is usually better to use the symbol type such as hairpins instead of 'crescendo' and 'diminuendo' and accents instead of '*sfz*', thus avoiding the danger of conflict with the text. For this reason barlines are usually placed through the stave only, and do not extend to join a whole system.

Accompaniment

The accompaniment, if there is one, will always be written below the voice parts (the position of voices in an orchestral score will be dealt with later). If there is no accompaniment, the composer would do well to consider adding an exact reduction on two staves that can be used by a pianist or organist in the rehearsal stage, marking this 'for rehearsal only'. A printer would usually set this in smaller type.

An independent accompaniment is almost always likely to be more elaborate than the vocal line it supports. Particularly in the writing of a solo song with keyboard accompaniment it is best to write the latter first, remembering to allow for any particularly long words and syllables of many letters. This process can be reversed if the accompaniment becomes very simple or dwindles out for a time. The method of writing the vocal notes and text simultaneously, though automatically taking care of the length of any word, has the danger of finishing up with the text written on a variety of planes. This can be guarded against by ruling guide lines in advance, and later erasing them, but the best position for these is not always seen until a line is finished. After a little experience it will be found best to add the words later, sufficient space having been 'automatically' allowed for them.

When writing on transparencies a text can fairly easily be added, last of all, using a typewriter—provided the sheet will fit into the carriage and care is taken not to smudge the already written work by too much winding on and back when it is in the locked position. The best density is obtained by backing the page with a sheet of carbon paper the 'wrong way round', thus producing an extra impression on the reverse of the page. It remains my view, however, that anyone who has developed a good enough hand to write musical characters should be able to write a freehand text satisfactorily; the fixed size of the type in the machine is not necessarily the best for every job. In addition, of course, the spacing between the letters is invariable.

A stave line left between voice and accompaniment will almost always be an essential; this will allow ample room for the text, and also accommodate any excursion into the higher registers by the accompaniment. Since in all probability a line will also need to be left between systems (depending a little on the left hand of the accompaniment) it will be seen that often no more will fit on to a twelve-stave page than on to a ten-stave one. Blank staves will probably be less necessary on a folio size twelve-stave page, but ideally fourteen staves on this type of page will allow three systems to be written with maximum clarity. Papers with special vocal rulings can be obtained; as with piano rulings, these should be investigated, and used if they suit one's personal style.

Spoken Texts

No further problems should be met with in the writing of the spoken texts found in various types of combination of speech and song. A purely spoken text requires no notes at all, of course, but the number of words spoken during a bar is often more than will fit easily into the space allowed by the music. It is not difficult to write several lines one beneath the other in the space of a bar of music; advance consideration of how many staves to leave around a narrator's part is recommended.

Rhythmic speech is usually indicated by notes without heads, or crosses in place of heads. The first, however, cannot show a value as long as a minim, and the second can show this value only with some modification, such as an actual minim crossed through.

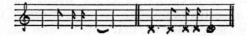

It is better to use regular notes, either placed on a single line or on a selected position on a stave with no clef (like unpitched percussion). Speech-song can be shown by using notes approximating to pitch (regular notes with crosses added in mid-stem) or by using a single line with notes placed on or near it according to the pitch required (sometimes used in conjunction with leger lines). I consider this method better applied to a stave without a clef.

Single lines can be 'manufactured' on pre-ruled paper by ruling the centre line of a stave into a much thicker one—or, in the case of transparencies, scratching them out from the reverse side of the paper. The works of Arnold Schoenberg in particular contain many examples of this type of writing (e.g., *Gurrelieder, Pierrot Lunaire, Survivor from Warsaw, Ode to Napoleon Bonaparte*).

(See also p. 114.)

CHAPTER EIGHT

Chamber Music

Solo Instruments and Piano

Music for solo instrument and piano differs little from that for solo voice and piano as far as committing to paper is concerned. A duo for violin and piano is set out in exactly the same way as a solo song, except that the words are no longer a problem, and the dynamics and other expression marks are now restored to their normal positions.

There is one more small difference, however, which will gradually lead us to the more complex problems of orchestral score and parts. The solo singer will almost invariably sing from a copy which contains the accompaniment—in other words a copy identical to that used by the accompanist. The violinist (or other instrumentalist) in a duo with piano will have just an extract—his own part only. In the first place he doesn't really need more, unless the piece is extremely complicated, and the full question of cueing will be examined later in Chapter 10. Whatever the pianist is playing, the way to produce a note on the violin is to put a finger on a definite point on the string; the singer is not so fortunate, and generally has to pitch a note by relation to what else is happening—hence, a visual reminder of what the pianist is doing is of immediate value.

Then, unless it is a very short piece fitting on to an open double page, the complete version will require the page to be turned at some point or other. The singer will have two hands free to do this at any time; the violinist almost certainly won't. It is not very likely that there will obligingly be a rest for the violin at the end of every right-hand page. So the violinist will need to have his own part only, which will contain much more on each page, making it easier for any page turns to be properly planned. (The unfortunate accompanist is left out of this arrangement, and must either cope alone or enlist the help of a page turner.)

Before all this is dismissed as too elementary to be worth mentioning, I must offer two cautionary tales on the provision of individual parts and page turns. Normally the more instruments that are involved in a piece, the easier it will be to find a page turn (i.e., a rest) in the music each one is playing. Not long ago I had to prepare a set of parts for a string quartet in which much of the tempo, points of entry, and style of performance of any one of the parts was governed by what was happening in the others. This called for the inclusion of much cueing—all condensed on to a single independent stave—even though the density of the piece meant that both violins at least had not as much as a bar's rest for quite some time from the start. The result was that, even though I wrote on large size paper with fourteen staves on it, both violin parts ran to five pages before a turn could be made. I managed to design a part which had all five pages open and visible at one time, by fixing the outer margins of pages two and three together and also four and five; I later heard that these fortunately did not fall off the music stands during performance, though how many stands each player needed to support that length of part I did not hear.

The second anecdote concerns a composer who insisted on a string quintet being played from scores rather than individual parts, in order that the players 'can see what each other is doing'. Poor things, they couldn't possibly have read more than two other lines at the most whilst coping with their own parts, and presumably the more difficult moments would have been afforded some rehearsal. In any case there was nothing that an individual part with a well written cue-line, as described later (page 95), would not have clearly shown. No rests in any of the parts were to be found at the end of any of the pages in the score, which needed to be turned after every fourth system of music, i.e. very often. I was just about to pronounce the situation as impossible when I heard that the players were to be provided with a page turner each. I still wonder what chance that piece had of being appreciated when it was accompanied by a ballet of five page turners jumping up and down every ten seconds or so, presumably in well-drilled unison.

To return to our instrumental duo for a few moments; if the solo instrument is a clarinet, for example, the problem of whether or not to transpose the part in the complete (i.e. pianist's) copy has to be considered. The pianist might well prefer the clarinet part in his copy to be written as it would sound, and if this copy is viewed as a piano part with clarinet cued in then perhaps all should be written as sounding. On the other hand, the complete copy is really a score of the complete piece and the pianist is just playing from a score; it is my view that proper transposition should be made as in any full orchestral score.

Instrumental Ensembles

The task of writing down chamber music for any number of performers differs hardly at all from writing an orchestral score, and the subsequent preparation of parts for the performers is an identical proposition. All the remarks in the following chapters on orchestral scores and parts apply to chamber music for any number of players. In its visual appearance on the page, a string quartet hardly differs at all from the string orchestra (other than the existence of a double bass line in post-classical works). The score layout for a chamber group should follow that of the orchestral score; the two most notable exceptions to this are the standard wind quintet, where the horn is usually written above the bassoon, most probably to have the bass clef part at the foot of the score, and works including a piano, when this instrument usually appears at the foot of all other parts. The temptation to arrange unusual ensembles by voicing should be resisted, as it will lead to all sorts of difficulties; a possible relaxation of this rule is when a solitary violin appears at the foot of a mixed ensemble; it might, though not necessarily, look better at the top of each system.

CHAPTER NINE

Score-Writing

With a few exceptions, which will be dealt with as they arise, a score is meant for reading, and not for playing from. It follows, then, that although nothing written in it should be ambiguous or uncertain, a number of accepted shorthand devices, 'short cuts', and similar practices may be adopted in writing a score which must be carefully avoided when extracting individual parts from it.

Layout of Page 1

The most accurately detailed orchestral score would have a single line for each instrument, as do most scores of chamber music works. The result, however, would be extremely cumbersome, and extremely difficult to take in at a glance. Like instruments are therefore grouped together, and share the same stave unless their parts become active enough to make it necessary for them to be shown separately. The first page of a score should be laid out for all the instruments to be involved in the work whether they play at the beginning or not. A less satisfactory, but still acceptable, alternative is to have a separate page detailing the entire orchestra (with doublings where they apply) and begin the first page of music only with those instruments actually playing.

The standard layout for a large orchestra with triple wind is as follows:

Piccolo
Flutes 1 & 2
Oboes 1 & 2
Cor Anglais
Clarinets 1 & 2
Bass Clarinet
Bassoons 1 & 2
Double Bassoon

Horns 1 & 2
Horns 3 & 4
Trumpets 1 & 2
Trumpet 3
Trombones 1 & 2
Trombone 3
Tuba

Timpani
Percussion

Harp

Violin 1
Violin 2
Viola
Cello
Bass

Simple variations on this will be dictated by necessity. The total number of staves to accommodate the above will depend on the number of percussion players involved, whether a blank stave is left above the first violins (a desirable practice, as it not only separates the strings clearly, and prevents high violin parts running into the bass of the harp, but also leaves sufficient space for adding tempo directions, rehearsal figures, etc.), and whether any further division on to separate staves is needed to allow for athletic clarinets, divided strings, and so on. It can be seen that the choice of twenty-four staves by many printers as a desirable full score size is quite arbitrary; twenty will normally accommodate a 'double wind' orchestra, and the larger orchestra nearly always needs as many as twenty-eight and often more.

Some slight alterations to the above are sometimes seen; if the piccolo is only occasionally played by the 3rd flautist, its part will appear beneath the other flutes (an exceptional instance of a predominantly higher member of a family being written in a lower position in the score). This may also be found if the 2nd or 3rd clarinettist occasionally plays the E♭ clarinet. Major departures, such as those adopted by Wagner (based on the actual voicing of parts) should be avoided; so should the modern practice of writing the horns below the trumpets as though they were alto members of the brass family. The tuba often shares a stave with the bass trombone, and I cannot help feeling that in many ways this has led composers to write for the instrument as though it were a trombone with an extended downward range. Any Wagner score will demonstrate otherwise. It is better to separate the two.

Any other instruments are inserted into the above layout according to their family positions, with saxophones as a group placed between bassoons and horns; a saxophone doubled by a clarinettist, however, would be written on the appropriate clarinet stave. All keyboards (and also guitar, mandolin, etc.) are grouped in the harp 'area'; the order does not really matter as long as like instruments (e.g., piano and celeste) are kept next to each other. Any solo concertante instruments are placed above the first violins (no longer between violas and cellos as was the case in many pre-twentieth-century scores); vocal parts occupy this position also, above the instrumental solo if there is one.

A final regular variation on the layout which is often found is the pairing of four horns as 1 & 3, 2 & 4. This has its origins in the fact that horns 1 & 2 took high and low notes respectively, and when two more horns were added to the orchestra they followed the same principle; horns 1 & 3 therefore take high notes, and horns 2 & 4 low ones. Purely as a matter of organization in a score, either method would seem to be equally acceptable except when the intervals between the notes of high and low players become very wide; in this case the pairing of 1 with 3 and 2 with 4 is more practical. Provided the score shows clearly which part is for which player, this is all that matters from a layout standpoint.

The title of the work should be placed centrally, the composer's name on the right, set lower than the title; this and any other necessary acknowledgements (from the authorship of texts to a copyright notice) may be seen in any classical printed score using such resources, with the likely exception of the copyright notice; this is placed at the foot of the page, sometimes centrally, better beginning at the left. A small word of warning is necessary with regard to using printed editions as models. Standard engraved editions almost certainly adhere to strictly correct engraving procedure, and make immaculate models. Many modern editions are prepared by other methods, from the finest autography to a facsimile of the composer's manuscript (not necessarily the extremes of good and bad). But however good such a production might be, most are liable to disregard some rule or other by accident or design, and should not be taken as foolproof examples of correct procedure.

Transposing

The actual notes written in a score may differ from those on the part before the player; this at first may seem astounding, and indeed the best method of writing a score is unquestionably to write the notes for transposing instruments duly transposed as the player will need them in his individual part. The alternative is to write everything in a score as it should sound, usually known as 'in C' or 'in concert'. (To avoid using many leger lines, however, piccolo, double bassoon, and double bass are usually transposed an octave as usual.) This method would seem to have no genuine advantage other than to promote laziness on the part of the writer; it is not quicker for an experienced hand to write than a properly transposed score. From a reading point of view it is easier to spot the clarinet line, for example, in a transposed score; indeed the very appearance of untransposed notes can look wrong to the eye trained to read a 'traditional' score. Horn parts, in particular, look very strange with their constant resort to the bass clef, and one composer not long ago admitted to me that writing in concert seemed to prompt him to write excessively high horn parts; this method often seems to go hand in hand with a lack of understanding of the qualities of tessitura of various instruments.

The methods of joining systems with brackets, etc., have already been dealt with in Chapter 3. Ideally each stave should carry its own appropriate clef, key signature, and time signature; abbreviations of the latter two by showing the top line correctly and drawing a line downwards from this through all lower staves till a variation is reached is not recommended. Several visual improvements on the sharing of time signatures may be seen, however. The best is probably a large signature drawn through all the staves of each family of instruments (treating timpani, percussion, and keyboards as one). This is immediately visible from any point in the score, whereas a single signature placed at the top and bottom of the page is not; a large signature placed centrally, cutting into a few staves, gives rise to some strange-looking spaces when all the notes at the beginning of a bar are vertically aligned. For all this, I must confess to a personal preference for the traditional method of one signature per stave, even though this may give rise to a great amount of work.

Bar lines should be drawn through family groups of wood-wind, brass, percussion, and strings, thus separating them for easy identification; timpani, keyboard instruments, etc. are barred individually. The single bar line from top to bottom of a system makes identification of a central instrument almost impossible. However laborious it may seem, silent bars should be filled with rests; an entirely blank bar gives an uneasy feeling of incompleteness. The rest is at least a guarantee that nothing has been left out (or should be!). Tempo indications and any subsequent changes should be written at the head of the score and additionally above the strings, but any further appearances are unnecessary.

Layout of Subsequent Pages

Two alternative layouts are available for page two and onwards of a score. Either the same principle of a full layout as on the first page can be maintained throughout, or the instruments not playing can be omitted. Not all instruments are likely to be called on constantly throughout a piece (or if they are it is hardly likely to be appreciated by either performer or audience); but in a short work of only a few minutes' duration the same page layout might well be kept for every page without the score becoming too bulky, or containing more empty bars than those with notes in them. Provided the layout is unchanged, there is no need to repeat the names of the instruments in the margins at all, though a sudden division of the strings or splitting of the flutes must be clearly indicated. The omission of clefs and key signatures from right-hand pages should, however, be confined to the sketchbook.

The reduction of the system to include only the instruments actually playing at the time is a far more satisfactory method. It is a little more time-consuming, in that it requires some advance planning, and each and every stave must bear the name of the instrument whose part it carries. It should be unnecessary to point out that the vertical order of instruments on a reduced system should be directly related to that of the full scoring, but a few years ago I conducted an opera by a composer—and a prominent one—who had obviously had to write his score in a great hurry. Although all the instruments playing in the first bar of any system were in the correct order, any that entered subsequently were merely added to the foot of the system as and when they entered. Thus it was not unusual to find a system with the order Flute, Bassoon, Trumpet, Violin, Clarinet, Cello, Oboe, followed by one with the order Oboe, Cello, Violin, Trumpet, Bass, Flute. That the composer had not the time to make a fair copy of his score is conceivable; that his publisher should not have bothered to do so, and should expect payment for such inadequate material, is not. One wonders how many subsequent performances have taken place.

The proper reduction of the system requires a little advance planning. If one is using 24-stave paper, it is obviously no use reducing a system to twelve staves if the following few bars are going to require thirteen staves. Some juggling with pencil and paper will repay any amount of time spent on it; one should not forget that with transparencies at least (and to a lesser extent opaque papers) it is not necessary to use the same stave ruling for every page, though a very striking change such as a page of twelve staves amongst a group with twenty-four should be avoided. Filling a short system with the string staves whether they play or not is a useful device for disguising a short page, but they should not appear and disappear at random. Occasionally one can get out of difficulties by including instruments which, although they may be silent, have something to play in the following system; an occasional full system just ahead of a tutti can also be used. Ideally, for the sake of clarity any page with more than one system should have them separated by both a blank stave and two short thick diagonal lines about 12 mm. long placed at (not in) either margin; these are often referred to as system breaks.

Sharing a line should be restricted to like instruments only (e.g., Oboes 1 & 2 but not Oboe and Cor Anglais); it must be absolutely clear in such cases 'who plays what'. If the notes are the same the indication 'a 2', 'a 3', etc., is normally sufficient. (This should be written in Italian and not French, i.e. without a grave accent.) Writing the stems up for one and down for two, as in normal part-writing, is usually clear in other cases; where both parts move in identical rhythms and have identical phrasing, single-stemming (like double-stopping) is permissible, but in this context the odd unison note can look awkward, even when given a head either side of the stem. The above possibilities should not be mixed within a phrase; the most apt should be selected and adhered to. The following example will display methods of leaving no doubt as to who plays which notes, though four horns are only likely to be found on one stave in an emergency.

Rests for the silent instruments are not necessary. Should a passage marked 'a 2' extend beyond a right-hand page, it should be marked again at the beginning of the new left-hand page.

A change of instrument (e.g., from Flute to Piccolo) should be marked as early as possible, and the new name repeated at the entry of the new instrument; the English word 'take' is even shorter than the Italian 'muta in'.

Similarly, muting and its opposite should be marked as early as possible and repeated at the relevant entry.

The latter half of these directions (unmuting) is frequently overlooked by composers. I offer no apology for the mixing of two languages above.

Alternative Notations

A number of abbreviations and other 'false notations' are permissible in a score, usually as labour-saving devices, but sometimes for the sake of clarity. It must be said, however, that all are in some way tiresome to the conductor. The most usual are a repeat sign, indicating that the bar containing it is the same as the previous one; and the indication that instruments written on different staves play the same notes for one or more bars. The simplest form might occur between violins.

In bar two the second violins repeat bar one; in bar three they play the same as the first violins (a wavy line through the stave sometimes replaces the symbol in bar three). It can be seen that a unison for full orchestra could be notated in such a fashion by writing a single bar of notes in one part and filling the others with symbols. Not recommended! A composer noted for his use of ostinato once pointed out that he composed music, not repeat signs; such practices should be confined to the sketchbook.

The octave signs can be employed freely in scores, and frequently need to be for reasons of vertical space, though their use in instrumental parts is severely restricted. During the writing of this book I was engaged on copying a score by a young composer who had used the symbols 𝄢 and 𝄢 for one and two octaves higher, and similar attachments to the bass clef. Although at first this seemed a sound idea in score-writing (though it would not do in individual parts) it soon became apparent that the pitch of any note was uncertain without looking back to the last clef used; in this unfortunate score the combinations of clef had become so confused, and often erroneous, that what was intended to be a unison often appeared as an octave or double octave between two instruments, and occasionally parts disappeared off the end of the instrument by nearly two octaves. The customary '8va' sign with its dotted line would have avoided all this: a clear case of novelty not being improvement.

A high passage for the bassoon or trombone, for example, might be written in a score in the treble clef, to avoid running into the stave above. (The tenor clef rarely saves using many leger lines in the extreme upper ranges of these instruments.) The copyist will, of course, have to restore such a passage to a clef acceptable to the player. Passages for divided strings may be written on one stave in a score, provided all movement of parts and directions for performance remain clear; in the parts, however, divisi should almost always take a stave to a part, unless they are of the very simplest nature. Performance directions such as a general crescendo for the entire orchestra need not be written into every stave; above the system and above the strings in a bold hand could be sufficient. When copying out parts, one must beware of these markings; they are easily overlooked. Identical dynamics and the like for similar groups of instruments on adjoining staves may be written between the staves and braced together.

The reappearance for a number of bars of an earlier moment in a score is sometimes represented by a single bar marked, e.g., A 1–8. This would mean repeat bars 1 to 8 of letter A as they appeared previously. Although a well understood and much used device, it should be kept to the sketchbook and to commercial scores, conductors of which are experienced in finding their way through any amount of such empty-looking occurrences. It is not to be used in normal circumstances.

Rehearsal Figures

All scores should be amply provided with reference points to aid rehearsal. For all extended works numbers are preferable to letters, which come round again after going through the alphabet. There are many systems in use, the two most satisfying being consecutive numbers placed at the beginning of significant bars, or alternatively, the actual bar number itself at such points. The latter version enables the parts to be checked more quickly for missing bars. The figure is usually placed in a box or a circle (a box is preferable since it uses less space). Its position on the score is the same as that for tempo indications, preceding them if they occur at the same bar, or written above if lack of space demands. They will not normally be necessary more frequently than ten bars or so, though in an exceptionally difficult work it may be helpful to number every bar (without a circle or box); conversely, not more than twenty or so bars should pass by without a reference. The very common practice of placing a figure exactly every ten bars has no value other than as a method of quickly calculating the number of bars in a piece, and as a means of checking parts for missing bars. In neither respect is it superior to the recommended method, and in any case rehearsal figures should be for a player's benefit, not a copyist's. This last method can sometimes be disturbing to the player; confronted by five seemingly equally important groups of ten bars rest, he may well hear significant happenings around him in bars 11, 19, 31, 41, and 49; the effect on one's confidence in one's ability to count can be quite demoralizing. A well-known opera contains an extended presto one-in-a-bar section, in which a rehearsal figure appears every five bars; it is quite a difficult task counting twenty groups of five silent bars (only a hundred in all, and past in less than a minute) all of which seem to be at rhythmic variance with what the other parts are doing (mostly four-bar phrases). 'Often but not too often' would seem to be the rule, and always at a significant point in the proceedings.

Smaller Groups

The layout of scores for smaller groups right down to the duo is no different from the order of an orchestral score, or should not be, with the exception of chamber works with piano, when

85

the piano customarily appears beneath all other instruments and also uses a score to play from; this is also true of vocal music and the duo-sonata. In larger chamber groups, particularly those needing a conductor, the piano usually retains its normal orchestral position.

Condensed Scores

Condensed scores and piano scores are merely reductions on to as few staves as possible of as much as possible of an orchestral score. Apart from possibly being cheaper to produce than a full score, they would seem to have little value except to a conductor who cannot read a score or a pianist who must fill in the parts of some missing instruments. The true piano reduction—an essentially playable version for the piano—has a definite value in the rehearsing of, for example, a choral work or an opera.

Another type of condensed score may be seen in the study score of Schoenberg's Violin Concerto. Although the layout in families is retained, all the notes for flutes (and similarly oboes, clarinets, etc.) are written on one stave whenever possible; additionally all the instruments involved in the many unisons characteristic of the composer's scoring often appear on one line. At one point within three bars the single line of notes on one stave is marked Cl.pic. Cl. a 2; Fl.1.2.3. Ob.1.2.3. Cl.pic. Cl. a 8; Fl.1.2.3. Cl.pic. a 4; Fl.1.2.3. Ob.1.2.3. Cl.pic. Cl. a 8. In addition to this, at the point where the oboes and clarinet drop out (and then return), notes in two different staves are beamed together. I was quite unsurprised to learn that a well-known conductor had had no choice but to write out an intelligible score for himself in traditional form in order to be able to rehearse the work properly.

Another innovation is to remove the stave altogether from the page when an instrument is silent (e.g. Stravinsky's *Mouvements* for piano and orchestra). Fortunately this is a very difficult and tiring process when writing manuscript. Its main effect is to make it almost impossible to identify an instrument at its entry; even when every little snippet of a stave has the instrument's name before it, this needs to be read and understood; most conductors will recognize a particular stave from its relation to others on the page; if they appear only spasmodically he cannot do so. The same conductor who 'rationalized' Schoenberg is known to have ruled in all the missing sections of stave in a score of this type. These two practices, when presenting music which can be written in the normal way (without loss to the result), have no function beyond making the music more difficult to read, and discouraging performers. (The full score of Wilfred Josephs' *Mortales* uses the last-mentioned method of incomplete stave lines as a means of explaining the construction of the first movement of the work, and as such may have some validity.)

What is delightfully termed a 'playing score', used in chamber music thought so difficult that each player must have a score to play from, to see what his fellow players are doing, will be discussed later, though the warning given previously (Chapter 8) should not be forgotten.

Percussion

A final word is necessary on the question of scoring for percussion. It should not be beyond the ability of the composer to decide how many players he needs, to allot instruments to each, and for the most part, at least, to stick to his plan; he will then avoid the addition of a ballet to his score, composed of percussionists rushing from one instrument to another and back again. Merely to write for the instruments without specifying players is to leave the task incomplete. He is leaving himself at the mercy of whoever copies out the parts (of which more later), or virtually giving carte blanche to every percussion section that plays his work. Elsewhere in his score the composer will most likely have been quite meticulous in specifying which player is to play the notes; in the percussion section, where such information is usually most needed, it is far too often lacking.

CHAPTER TEN

Part-Writing $\left(\text{I} \right)$

in general

Although the following notes will deal mainly with the making of orchestral parts from a score, they apply also to any type of part-copying. The same principle should govern everything— to present the composer's intentions in as clear, exact, and helpful a manner as possible.

Preliminary Checking

Before beginning to copy parts from a score some preliminary work will always be necessary. It may not always be stated (though it certainly should be) whether or not a score is properly transposed or 'in concert'; in fact the former should be assumed if nothing is noted. It is as well to check for a unison between transposing and non-transposing parts (such as clarinet and violins) or an exceptional use of bass clef for the horns if there is any uncertainty which cannot otherwise be resolved. Scores 'in concert' often do not specify keys for transposing instruments; it is unwise to assume automatically that the clarinets should be written in Bb. I learnt this the hard way, by once making such an assumption, and finally encountering a low C sharp on about page 90 of the score; check first, and if there are any such notes this passage at least must be written in A. It is probably as well to write the entire part in A under such circumstances unless the work is sufficiently tonal to demand the Bb instrument. The eight changes from A to Bb and back within the third movement of Michael Tippett's 2nd Symphony are not the sort of thing that the non-clarinet-player is likely to spot the need for. He will appreciate, however, that at the point in the score of the same composer's opera *The Midsummer Marriage* where change from A to B♭ is asked for in the middle of a passage without rests, some adjustment must be made.

It is becoming standard practice to write trumpet parts in C, though in educational and band music they should certainly be transposed into B♭. The transposing ability of clarinettists, trumpeters, and horn players too, in symphony orchestras is phenomenal, but this is no reason for trading on it.

Page Turns

Lengthy passages during which it would be impossible to turn a page should be looked for: fortunately these are only likely to be encountered in the strings, as the nature of other instruments demands either breathing space for the player or aural relief for the audience. Traps are set by composers, however; in Shostakovich's 7th Symphony the side drum plays some 350 bars without a rest—a similar case to Ravel's *Bolero*. Elaborate passage work for a clarinet, and more particularly the flute, with its constant use of leger lines, will always need advance planning. A work for string orchestra alone is likely to present great page-turning problems; it is best to select likely points in the score where a turn could be made, and plan the entire part from there in advance. A long passage likely to cover two pages can be a focal point from which to plan outwards; it is not always immediately obvious whether a part should best begin on page 1 or 2 (i.e. a right- or left-hand page). Remember, too, that a passage for violins divided into six may only occupy two staves in a score, but in a part this can easily expand to over a page. Having made a plan for such an instance, keep to it; there will be a temptation, if a page turns out to be shorter than calculated, to fit a little more in before making a turn; but if the planning has been well done, this is almost certain to upset something later on. Page turns in the strings are made by the second player at each desk. Occasionally in a divisi passage it may be necessary for the first player to make the turn (if he has more 'rests' than the second); an instruction to do so is necessary in the part.

It is often said that, because there are two players to each string desk, page turns do not matter, or matter less. This is quite untrue: the aural effect of half a section stopping playing whilst the other half struggles across a page turn will never pass unnoticed. Even if the first two or three bars of the new page are duplicated at the foot of the old one (when they must be very clearly marked), thus allowing the turn to be 'staggered', the result is hardly less obvious. Proper advance planning can usually remove the need for such bad turns. A very short or even entirely empty right-hand page is preferable to a bad turn; in any case one should never begin a right-hand page without deciding where the page turn is to come. A page may be extended by fixing an additional one to the outside margin, a device which can be repeated ad inf. A large spread of four or five pages, however, is quite likely to fall off the stand (see Chapter 8), and the left extremities are barely readable by the player sitting on the right, and vice versa. Such a part takes a little longer to turn when this point is eventually reached. The accordion fold type of binding (with music printed on one side of the paper only, and fastened at the edges, making it possible to see any number of pages at once in theory) does not solve this problem; in any case there is always somebody who manages to drop the unstable result, sometimes with disastrous consequences. In cases of extreme emergency, a silent player in the 'wind' section can turn a page for his partner; information in both parts at the necessary point is essential. There isn't much music, however, that will not reveal a page turn after twenty lines or so—the most unobliging are usually baroque-type continuo parts and jazz rhythm sections (virtually the same thing), and the few 'artful dodges' mentioned here should only be employed if no other solution is at all possible; as a means of covering some faulty planning, or lack of any planning at all, they should not be permitted. One further word of warning about the other end of the scale; avoid if possible a page turn in a G.P. (totally silent) bar. One or two instruments may turn if absolutely necessary, but it is not difficult to imagine the horrifying cumulative effect if, for instance, the entire orchestra were to turn a page hurriedly at the silent bar after the climax of Strauss's *Don Juan*.

It is not possible to say how many empty bars are necessary to ensure a good page turn. Time, and other actions involved, are what matters; a tuba player cannot turn a page as easily as a flute player, and if he also has to find his mute in the process quite a few bars are necessary. Three empty bars of $\frac{5}{4}$ at a speed of ♩=120 pass more quickly than a single $\frac{2}{4}$ bar at ♩=60 ; even when the latter has a crotchet on the first beat there is still more time for a turn. It is true that the psychological effect of a number of bars is more reassuring than that of one not even entirely empty, but this is not a practical consideration. Obviously, each individual case must be looked at on its merits (and otherwise). The addition of the letters 'V.S.' (volti subito—turn quickly) to the foot of a page or where the music ends is helpful when it is a necessary act; it should not be applied indiscriminately. Similarly, 'time to turn' is a helpful addition when there is indeed time to do so; this is particularly useful when the actual music runs right to the end of the page, to remind the player that it does not continue immediately on the next.

Silent Bars

Unless an instrument is silent throughout an entire movement, the word 'tacet' should not be used. A resting part should be a detailed map of what is taking place; over a long period of rest a couple of well-chosen melodic cues are all that is needed, with a little more detail approaching the actual entry. In a case of resting through a passage of constantly changing time signatures this unfortunately means a lot of work; I think that it was copying such a piece, and ending with three pages of nothing but rests almost entirely in single bars of different metres, that caused me to give up writing the figure 1 over a single empty bar.

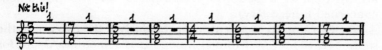

Cues

Cues in all parts are an absolute essential, unless the instrument concerned plays through a piece with virtually no rests. They have more than one function, though their primary one is to assure the player that his counting of rests is going correctly; they can also be of assistance to a player or singer in pitching a difficult note. Some cues are built into parts automatically; a new tempo, for example, is likely to be recognized immediately, even if it follows as many as 200 bars rest; the sudden interpolation of a $\frac{5}{8}$ bar into a section of otherwise constant $\frac{2}{4}$ can hardly be missed. Other cases in the form of notes must be selected by the copyist from the score. A good method is to imagine oneself playing the part and to ask not only 'what would I like to hear' at any point, but also 'what am I likely to hear?' A good cue may not always be obvious from a mere glance at the score; a silent 3rd trombone, however, is certain to hear or be aware of an entry by the 2nd trombone, even though it may be the quietest pianissimo, and quite inaudible to the flutes. Ideally a cue should be a melodic one, from an instrument either playing a solo or having just made an entry; these, of course, are not always available. The entry of a section or part of a section of the orchestra can be shown by a group name beneath the bar concerned; all cues should bear the name of the instrument playing them, and must also be written in the key of the instrument they are intended to help. A flute cue, for example, written into a horn part must be transposed as though the horn were to play it; care must be taken over double transposition—a B♭ clarinet cue in a horn part will be written only a fourth higher than it actually appears in the clarinet part (where it is already transposed one tone). It is customary to ignore octave transpositions, however; a piccolo part written in to a horn part as if the horn were to play it would all be on leger lines; for convenience of reading, the notes and not the octave higher sound are written as a cue (duly transposed for the instrument concerned if necessary).

Cueing right up to an entry, particularly if the two are in the same bar, should be avoided though it is sometimes useful for showing the continuity of a phrase; filling the short rests in an active part with cues is nothing but confusing. As already stated, the cue is written in small notes, preferably always with stems up, and all the rules of spacing are observed; that is, everything else, including the length of the bar on the stave, is reduced proportionately. Leger lines, however, remain the same distance apart (though they will be shorter). If they didn't, there would be much confusion where cue and entry met; in any case the leger line is really an extension of the stave, which is not reduced in size. Where the cue and an entry meet in the same bar, it will be necessary to extend the horizontal spacing of the cue to accommodate full-size rests in the main part.

The following example shows a number of types of cue.

At figure 1 the oboes enter; what they play may be assumed to be something of no further help if it were actually notated. The bassoon cue later is sufficiently melodic to be written in;

since all rehearsal figures must be shown whether the player is resting or not the ensuing four bar rest has to be split up to show figure 2. Some cue after the eighteen bars rest at figure 3 would normally be a help, but both a new time signature and a new tempo make figure 4 immediately recognizable. The viola cue in bar four of figure 5 is to assist the horn in pitching the low B after playing at the top of the register. Brass players and horn players in particular need to be able to 'hear' a note in the head before accurately producing it (unlike the pianist, who merely depresses a key), and although there is no need to litter a part with 'helpful' pitches, a sudden change of tessitura such as the above is definitely simplified by the cue here. The final cue shows the meeting of cue and entry in the same bar, also involving leger lines.

A vocal cue in an opera orchestral part, though often seen, is not normally of much use, as it is unlikely to be heard from the orchestra pit; furthermore, the orchestra will begin rehearsals alone, and by the time the singers join them, the work should be fairly well learnt. A significant phrase from the stage, when the orchestra is silent or pausing, or when the dramatic needs of the stage might affect the flow of music, can make a helpful cue. Because of this last effect, opera parts need to be well cued during rests.

Cueing down, that is, writing additional notes in a part to be played if the instrument they were originally intended for is not available (or cannot manage them) is done in one of two ways. For example, when cueing an oboe part into a clarinet part (remember to transpose!), if the clarinet is silent, the oboe line should be written as a normal cue, though certainly large enough to be properly read. If the clarinet has to abandon its own part, however, and play the oboe part instead, the new part should be written on a separate stave above the original; if they are put on the same stave, as sometimes seen, clarity is always sacrificed. The practice of writing such cues in different coloured ink (usually red, which retains its individuality under artificial lighting) is of no value in work for reproduction.

Except in the instances just mentioned, it is not normal to include any marks of expression in cues; merely the notes will be sufficient, though an occasional phrase mark can give added character and point to a cue. Any cue that might have to be played, however, requires all the indications applied to the original.

Chamber music parts for works without a conductor often benefit from a little more cueing than those in which a conductor may presumably be relied upon for help with a difficult entry; the probable presence of a conductor, though, must not be an excuse for not cueing a part properly. But the 'playing score' mentioned earlier, though often suggested by composers and publishers, is rarely welcomed by players. The first point about such an instance is that if the work is difficult enough for the idea to be considered, it is likely that the performers will have to spend some time studying it; provided a score is available to be looked at when necessary, there is no need for the ensemble to play from one in performance. A string quartet asked to play from a score will in the first instance be turning pages nearly four times as often as if they had individual parts, and it is not very likely that turns suitable for all four players can be constantly and frequently found (see Chapter 8). Additionally, each player will have three other staves to distract his attention, at least two of which will most likely be in clefs other than his own; the assumed difficulty of the work means that he could probably do without these distractions.

However complicated the music may be there is nothing that cannot be achieved by the use of one single cue stave above the player's own part; the use of it need not be continuous, in fact, it should be reserved for displaying essentials. However free the music may be, the player will need to know when to begin his part (usually when another instrument reaches a certain point) and when to stop (which may be related to a similar occurrence). What happens whilst he is actually playing is of lesser significance; in fact unless it is definitely affected by what another player does, his part should show no cues. The intelligent reduction on to one extra stave of the essentials is far superior to the provision of a score, and leaving the players to select for themselves what matters.

The Clarinet Concerto by Thea Musgrave shows many

applications of these principles, and in fact the score will repay much study, since it raises many of the problems of the preparation of orchestral parts. At various times during the concerto an instrument will be led either by the conductor, or by the solo clarinettist (sometimes in direct opposition to the conductor), or will even take its entries from another single instrument, and pass on the same, without reference to any other players. A simple instance may be seen on page 25 of the score, figure 22.

A first glance at the woodwind parts might suggest that none of them is going to be able to place an entry correctly, or finish playing at the right moment, without having the entire page of score before them. But, for example, all the cor anglais part need show on a cue stave is the bassoon part, which will show when to begin playing, and then the beginning of the oboe part, showing when to stop; nothing else is necessary. Similarly the oboe cue line will show only the flute part (after an appropriate pause); the final bar is indicated by the conductor—the bracketed pause shows that the oboe must hold the note until the lead is given for the D. The fact that around all this, in the oboe's case, are similar free passages for bassoon and cor anglais is unnecessary information, though it could be added by including these instruments' names, as in the first cue in the example on page 93. But additionally the solo clarinet has its own entirely free solo, which continues throughout and affects the conductor's indication of the last bar; furthermore the conductor and the string section (plus horn and double bassoon) continue in yet another, strict tempo of their own. All of this information could be given in the oboe part, verbally or with cue staves; not one bit of it is going to help him place his solo any more accurately than the single flute cue. This matter will be dealt with further in Chapter 13.

Finally, there are moments when one must wonder whether all one's efforts to help the player with cues are worth while. Most orchestral musicians are capable of counting hundreds of empty bars faultlessly; I have sat during a rehearsal with a percussion section which carried on a sotto voce conversation on the sports results throughout a silent portion of a work which consisted of many uneven bars and no cues at all.

The entire section suddenly stopped conversing and began playing at exactly the right moment, without even a nod from the conductor. On the other hand, no player can be expected to play in the right place if confronted by 'tacet to fig. 83', when his part begins again exactly at fig. 83 with a flurry of notes. (I have seen, and played from, such a part.) And yet, having once given a wind player what I thought was a helpful cue only eight bars after the beginning of an Allegro section (for an entry in bar 14) I later found that he had pencilled over the cue 'count like hell'. The only advice I can offer is to persevere with intelligence and good intentions.

All instruments should have their own part; double wind parts will be discussed later in the chapter on Time-Saving, but in general this practice should be given up. Whilst player 1 is actually playing he will not particularly want to know what player 2 is doing (such problems as ensemble aside) and may not necessarily be able to hear it anyway. In the percussion section this may not always be possible, but, provided the composer has laid out his music properly, players generally prefer just their own part to a composite score of the whole section's music. Although it is sometimes said that the players would prefer a score, in order to work out amongst themselves who is to play what, this is just not so (and, in any case, is the composer's duty). One should no more consider giving such a task to the percussion section than, for example, giving a score of four horn parts to the four players, and leaving them to sort out their own individual lines.

CHAPTER ELEVEN

Part-Writing (2)

in particular; and some specific notation

Strings

The copying of orchestral parts from a score should always begin with the strings. They are likely to be more employed than the other parts, and by the time the copyist has completed these parts he will have been through the score thoroughly five times, and should have a good idea of the construction of the work. This will be invaluable in copying the other parts, though he should not forget that even if he has learnt the work, the players have not, and he should not fall into the trap of writing fewer and fewer cues as he goes along.

Any indication to play in a particular style, e.g. 'sul tasto', 'con sord.', 'pizz.', etc., must be placed over the first note to which it applies, or immediately before if space so demands. As mentioned previously, sufficient warning must be given if the indication requires some physical action, such as putting on a mute. A return to normal is also noted above the first note to which it applies; 'ord.' is sufficient to cancel unusual

bowing instructions. It will not do to write a cancellation at the end of an unusual passage.

The use of a dotted line from a direction such as 'sul pont.' is unnecessary if a cancellation word is used; a direction to play on a particular string is best noted and cancelled as follows:

Sometimes, if a direction continues over many lines, it may be as well to add a reminder of its continuance at a strategic moment, particularly if there might be a doubt whether the instruction holds good or not. For example, the first violins might have sixteen bars of pizzicato, followed by a few bars rest; they then resume playing pizzicato, but are joined by the second violins playing arco. A bracketed direction (sempre pizz.) will obviously be a great help, though in such an extreme case the composer should have provided it himself.

Divided string passages can often raise problems in layout. Generally a simple division into octaves or other constant intervals can be written on one stave with both heads on the same stem, like double-stopping—one need have no fear of the players attempting to play individually in octaves unless so marked; the abbreviation 'div.' should be added, however. It will be found that a little more space is required than for a single line of notes. Even a short passage in which the rhythm of each part varies may be written on one stave with separate stemming, provided it can be kept absolutely clear; each part should have its own phrasing, etc., though dynamic markings can be shared. Otherwise a division must be written out with a stave to each part, bracketed together, and bar lines drawn right through the system. It is unlikely that such a passage will be so obliging as to begin at the beginning of the copyist's stave or end at the end of one, though it is possible to arrange this on occasions; hence some duplicating of the odd unison bars will usually be needed. It will not do to write 'col 1' in the second or other parts, as in scoring, leaving the players to jump from one line to another. A return to a single line of notes on a single stave is best marked 'unis.' (not 'a 2'), but

the practice of giving a warning at the end of a previous line
by drawing a brace and writing 'unis.' or adopting a similar
procedure at the end of a single line for a subsequent division
should be discontinued.

A sudden change from a division into two to one into three
and back again is a copyist's nightmare; no amount of juggling
will permit it to be written so as to ensure that every player
has a continuous stave. String players normally divide at the
desk for div. in 2 (that is, one player at each desk to a part);
larger divisions are usually made by desks, both players at
any one desk playing the same part. Thus it will be seen from
the following example, which is an accepted way of writing a
changing division (and seems to me to be the best) that the
unfortunate 1st player on desks 3 and 6 has to read from line
one to line three and back again.

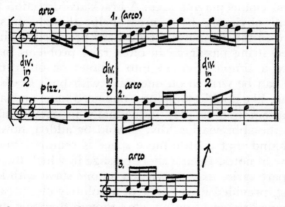

In a simpler case, a triple division can be accommodated on two
lines, though a part should not wander from one line to another.

If the composer has written his division on one stave, it is quite likely that any accidentals are not carried through both parts, and care must be taken to ensure that all separate staves in the parts are correctly notated. Solo parts within the section are written on a separate stave above the main body (unless the latter are silent)—the words 'cogli altri' may be added at the end of a solo passage to avoid duplicating bars of unison, particularly if the exact point at which the solo rejoins the main body is not specified.

Double sharps and double flats should not be written in string music; a G double-sharp, for example, has to be fingered by the player as an A and not impossibly stretched for from below. Passages such as that working into E sharp major in the opening pages of Wagner's *Siegfried Idyll* are invariably 'transposed' by the players. It is a brave man who will change such a symbol if the composer has written one, but such a move will almost certainly be appreciated by the players concerned.

Phrase slurs and bowing slurs are represented by the same symbol; whether to include both in a score (which can often be confusing) or which to exclude is a matter for the composer, and may well be bound up with his particular style. To omit both, however (as often happens with the tremolo and the glissando, for example), is as much a failure as omitting accidentals or other expression marks. The copyist cannot supply them and they will have to be worked out in rehearsal by the unfortunate players. Whilst not attempting to explain compositional techniques, I must strongly discourage the use of

♩ ♩ ♩ ; its regular appearance in scores suggests that its ambiguity

is not recognized. If a slurred triplet is required it should be

written ♩ ♩ ♩ ; if no slurring is required it should written be

without the slur. Neither style is deducible from the first example; the use of a slur instead of a bracket with the figure invariably causes confusion.

Violin parts need a lot of space; two leger lines either side of the stave are necessary to encompass the most elementary positions; add to these the sparsest performance directions above and below, and the need to keep the next stave in mind when copying will be obvious. One should not hesitate to leave a blank stave when necessary, rather than be forced to cramp the notes of two staves together, or destroy horizontal spacing to avoid this. Avoid using the '8va' sign if possible, though because the stave lines are already ruled this cannot always be done; passages up to C above the fifth leger line are easily read if properly written.

Viola parts should be kept in the alto clef wherever possible— Beyond the first octave of the A string, however, the treble clef will be used; the alto clef should be restored as soon as possible.

The cello uses three clefs, principally the bass clef, though most A string music fits better in the tenor clef. For the extreme upper range the treble clef is used, but it should be avoided if the tenor clef plus a few leger lines can be used instead; constant jumping from one clef to another must be avoided at all costs. The practice of writing in the treble clef an octave higher than actual sound is, or should be, obsolete, though it can still be seen in the scores of Bruckner, for instance. The cellist cannot turn the page as quickly as the violinist.

The double bass uses the same three clefs as the cello, though sounding an octave lower than written; the use of the tenor and treble clefs is much rarer. Notes written in these two clefs were once also intended to sound an octave lower than written, but with the contemporary extension of double bass technique to include the use of a higher register, it has become simpler to write treble (and tenor) clef music at pitch. Music using these clefs needs to be accompanied by an explanation of what pitch is meant to be heard. It will be seen, however, that by using the 'at pitch' method the need for leger lines is virtually removed. The bass player always needs a little time to turn the page, since he must sit some distance from the desk; his part, too, needs to be written in a bold enough hand to be seen from this distance.

Woodwind and Brass

It is quite usual for two (sometimes more) instruments to share a stave in the score. When extracting parts, exceptional care must be taken to ensure that all performance directions down to the smallest staccato dot are written into each individual part.

Tonguing is as important a part of wind playing as bowing is of string playing; the inclusion of the phrase slur in addition to the slurs indicating tonguing and breathing in wind music can often produce an over-emphasized style of playing that the composer did not intend. Though it must remain a matter for the individual composer, the phrase slur is often best considered expendable. A slur over a group of notes will be interpreted by a wind player as a single phrase; put in crudest terms, a single uninterrupted blow. The absence of a slur will indicate separate articulation of the notes; not a separate blow for each, but the flow of air regulated by the action of the tongue. Between these two lie a multitude of different attacks, of which it is necessary to detail the notation of double- and triple-tonguing. They are distinguished from each other as follows.

It will be seen that it is not possible to notate triple-tonguing in this manner in notes of the value of a minim or more, but once the notation has been established for a bar or so, the crotchets in the above example can be replaced with a dotted minim and the dots and slurs by 'sim.'. The addition of a time dot to the notes to be triple tongued, though often seen, is utterly incorrect and illogical.

Flutter-tonguing (like a continuously rolled 'r') is written as a one note tremolo; the addition of the German abbreviation 'flz.' (flatterzunge) is helpful and readily understood.

Use of the trill sign in conjunction with the word, or a wavy
line only in place of the tremolo marking, is not recommended;
neither is the letter 'z' written through the stem—not possible
in unstemmed notes. This latter notation was used by Berg to
denote quarter-tones (Zwischentönen—'between-tones').

As with other instruments there is the same need to warn of
muting and its cancellation in advance, and to mark it on
appearance; cancellation is often overlooked by composers,
and many a copyist has come across a work in which
instruments are apparently muted all through owing to such
an oversight. Muting, incidentally, is possible on some woodwind instruments, though it is to be hoped it would not be used
by a composer who did not understand its implications; a note
of explanation in score and part is really necessary.

Hand muting on the horn is represented by a '+', a sign
also used for the 'key-click' in woodwind instruments. (If used
on the horn this latter device requires an explanation, and not
the '+' symbol.) Hand muting is cancelled by the symbol 'o';
when used for any number of successive notes a line of '+'s
looks rather foolish and it is better to mark the passage
'chiuso'—this will be understood to hold good until cancelled
by 'aperto'. The half-stopped note on the horn is represented
by the + enclosed in a circle; the result is rarely more than a
note of seemingly uncertain intonation.

A few simple notes on the copying of parts follow.

Flutes. Music for the flute family will generally involve much
use of leger lines. For this reason a paper with plenty of space
between the staves is necessary, and it will soon be discovered
that music involving many leger lines also requires more
lateral space than that lying between the staves. (This is
because a space must separate the extremes of the lines rather
than merely the note-heads.) As far as possible the '8va' sign
should be avoided; excursions beyond top C for the flute are
rare, though a case such as the top F (Boulez, *Sonatina*) requiring
seven leger lines would probably be impossible to write on
pre-ruled paper. The temptation to use the '8va' sign for
passages such as the opening of the Ritual Dances from Michael
Tippett's opera *The Midsummer Marriage* should be firmly

resisted; provided the leger lines are properly spaced, such a passage presents no reading problems (only copying problems!). Cues in a piccolo part should be written as they sound; the same is true of the very rare bass flute in C—octave transpositions are normally disregarded when writing cues. What is often called the bass flute—the alto flute—is pitched in G and the normal transposition rules apply.

Oboes. Parts will normally lie within the stave or just above, with a few virtuoso exceptions, making the use of the '8va' sign unnecessary. The cor anglais uses only the treble clef; although Russian scores in particular notate the part in the alto clef, this cannot be used in the player's part, and in fact has not much value in scoring either as it often involves many leger lines. Parts for the rare bass oboe have been written in both the bass clef (Delius, *Dance Rhapsody No. 1*) and the treble clef, sounding an octave lower (Holst, *The Planets*); from the player's point of view this latter would seem preferable, in which case cues should be written as they sound.

Clarinets. Parts for all instruments of the clarinet family are best written in the treble clef; 'German notation' for the bass (and contrabass) clarinet, that is, writing a second away from the actual sound in the bass clef (a ninth away for the contrabass) is not recommended, although still sometimes found. This will mean an occasional use of many leger lines for the lowest notes; the '8va' sign below or above should not be used for any of the instruments. The exceptional range of all the instruments of the family will mean constant employment of leger lines; the remarks concerning the violins apply equally here. Cues for those instruments transposing beyond an octave should not themselves be transposed out of their sounding octave.

Bassoons. Parts for both bassoon and double bassoon should be written in the bass clef wherever possible (the tenor clef is never really necessary for the double bassoon because of the limit to its upward range). Three leger lines present no trouble to a player, though passages such as the opening of Stravinsky's

Rite of Spring must obviously be written in the tenor clef. The '8va' sign is never used, nor is the treble clef, even for the top Es of Wagner's *Tannhaüser* Overture, or Ravel's Piano Concerto (though it may be used in a score for sheer convenience). Cues for the double bassoon should sound as written.

Saxophones. All saxophone music is written in the treble clef, duly transposed to B♭ or E♭ as appropriate. Remote keys are often encountered in both transpositions and key signatures should be used where possible to facilitate reading.

Horns. As far as possible horn parts should be written in the treble clef. The noted composer and horn player Gunther Schuller, in his book *Horn Technique*, recommends the use of the treble clef down to low C; reasons of spacing, however, sometimes make it necessary for a passage written in this low tessitura to be notated in the bass clef. As in the treble clef such a passage should be written a fifth higher than sounding. A note to this effect should be included in the part, however, since the older 'German' notation of writing bass clef parts a fourth lower than they sound is still met in many classical orchestral parts; if the bass clef is only used for notes beyond low C this method merely extends the use of leger lines. A constant change of clef for a passage in the 'tenor' register is to be avoided at all costs, even if it means a few notes on leger lines above the bass clef stave. The '8va' sign is never used.

Traditionally, horn parts are written without key signatures, a relic of the days when horn music was always written in C, and the instrument 'crooked' into the appropriate key of the piece. The majority of modern music is not written with key signatures, so the question of using them or not hardly arises. My own view, shared with most horn players, is that they should not be used.

Trumpets. Parts should always be written in the treble clef, without the use of the '8va' sign; the use of the bass clef (Mozart, *Don Giovanni* Overture; Strauss, *Till Eulenspiegel*) has nothing but curiosity value. It is becoming modern practice to write all trumpet parts in C and to leave transposition and, indeed, the choice of instrument to the player; in parts which use either extreme of register this is a sound practice, and may well be adopted for all writing other than band and educational music, in which B♭ is an obligatory key. Key signatures are more often found in trumpet parts than horn parts; again, much modern writing renders them inappropriate, though I prefer to see them in diatonic music.

Trombones. For orchestral purposes parts are written in either the bass or, less often, the tenor clef; the alto clef, found as late as in the Symphonies of Schumann and Brahms, and also in modern Russian scores, should no longer be used. The general tessitura of the part will determine which clef is more suitable; a mixture of the two should be avoided if possible—an occasional high B♭ written in the bass clef is easily read, though if the part stays that high for any length of time, of course, the tenor clef should be used. (Such a passage might even appear in a score in the treble clef for space reasons, but this must be changed when copying a part.) Low notes in the tenor clef are best avoided, and the '8va' sign is never used, not even for the lowest pedal notes.

Tuba. The only likely problem in copying a tuba part is a constant use of leger lines, something like a violin in reverse. A great deal of lateral space will be needed; the part should be written in a fairly large hand as the player must sit some distance from the copy. Time is also necessary to cope with a page-turn comfortably. The '8va' sign should not be used if possible, but is occasionally useful for passages of a continuously low nature, to avoid having the notes run into the stave below.

Timpani and Percussion

The composer owes it not least to himself to organize his percussion writing properly. He should not find it difficult to settle on a given number of players and allot various tasks to them. If a number of keyboard-type instruments (e.g. xylophone, glockenspiel, etc.) are to be used, it is almost always a good idea to allot one to each player; similarly, each player should be responsible for a particular selection of instruments and not be expected to go running around from one spot to another in search of a triangle or drum just used by another player seated some five or six yards away. Some occasional duplication may be necessary, of course; a player cannot be expected to play the xylophone and side-drum simultaneously, even if he is otherwise totally responsible for these two instruments; another player can take over one temporarily, or even have a second instrument if preferred.

A composer who writes merely for instruments, rather than for a player handling an instrument, is heading for trouble. His copyist can, if he dares, sort out the score and do what the composer should have done in the first place (in which case the latter can hardly complain if he does not like the result). Or he can group certain instruments together, such as bass drum, cymbals, and triangle, and write a part containing their music only. This will not necessarily be handled by one player, or be the best grouping; in any case the resultant number of separate parts will not necessarily equal the number of players required. The percussion parts of many large-scale romantic works are produced in this way—the symphonies of Mahler, for instance; and parts which have been used by orchestras are covered in pencilled alterations transferring one or other instrument to one part or another. There are two further alternatives available to the copyist; he can make a part for each instrument, in which case he may well end up with twenty-six separate parts of no real use to the few players available; or he can make a score of all the happenings in the percussion section and leave the players to sort things out for themselves. Such a part is likely to have very many pages and to need constant turning (points for which can be very difficult to find); it can be no surprise if a player required to play only the fourth and tenth line of each page sometimes gets lost, or plays the wrong line. Whenever possible, one part per player is the satisfactory solution, and this is only properly achieved if the composer lays out his music so in the first place.

Unless one is prepared to rule one's own paper, the quite logical practice of writing on single lines for unpitched instruments must be abandoned. A number of instruments can share a five-line stave, however, provided they do not jump around from one line or space to another; as long as they are clearly marked on their first entry no more identification should be necessary, their position on the stave identifying them. All instruments should be named as they enter and as a change is required from one to another; additionally, in the parts (though not necessarily in the score) advance instructions on any change must be given, provided there is space to do so; the distinction between 'take' and 'to' should be obvious.

A normal clef, nearly always treble, is used for pitched instruments though the bass clef is used exclusively for the timpani and sometimes for the lowest notes of the marimba and vibraphone. A negative type of clef is usual for unpitched instruments, that in the following example being common; use of treble and bass clefs for unpitched instruments is meaningless and can lead to confusion in score-reading. A busy percussion part might look like this:

Assigning a specific line of a stave to one particular instrument can reduce the need for continuous naming of instruments.

The practice of replacing the names of instruments with diagrams or symbols seems to me fraught with danger, as is, for example, writing triangle parts with triangular shaped notes. The different symbols used for each percussion instrument are known only to the specialist composer and performer: such scores and parts are almost invariably annotated by conductors and performers with the proper names of the instruments.

Key signatures are not generally used in pitched percussion parts, and would of course be meaningless in unpitched parts. All accidentals should be written in as and when required; this warning is particularly directed at the timpani part—the practice of naming the tuning but omitting the accidentals is no longer permissible. The still older practice of treating the timpani as transposing instruments is hardly likely to arise.

A roll on the timpani or an unpitched instrument should be written as a trill, and not a tremolo, with its implied measured repetition. A new attack requires a new note-head and a new trill sign (though an internal accent may be shown merely with the appropriate symbol without breaking the trill). If the roll is continuous through many notes one trill sign is sufficient, though the note-heads may also be tied as a safeguard; the effect of a dotted tie is purely psychological. From the above it can be noted that what one often hears from the timpani at the end of the introduction to Dvořák's 'New World' Symphony is not what appears in the score.

Rolls on unpitched instruments often extend over many bars, as do other rhythmical patterns; anything extending beyond three bars should certainly have the bars numbered, centrally above, as a guide to the player. A roll between two timpani or other instruments is written as a broken tremolo and not a 'double-stopped' tremolo or trill.

The trill sign for a pitched instrument, however, means just that, and if a tremolo or roll on one note is required it should be written as such in the normal manner.

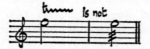

The correct notation for a sound left vibrating (the initials 'l.v.' denote the words in a number of languages) as opposed to one with a definite point of completion is a note filling a bar, tied incompletely into as many bars as it seems probable the sound will continue; the bars should be left empty and not filled with rests; such 'empty' bars should invariably be numbered.

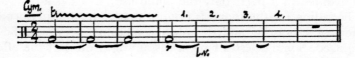

The omission of the note from a number of bars of continuous roll however, should remain an abbreviation for the sketch book.

The xylophone and glockenspiel usually sound respectively one and two octaves higher than written; this is not always so, however, particularly with the larger glockenspiel, and a note should always be included in score and part as to what pitch is intended. '8va' signs may be used for pitched percussion, though very sparingly; the reason for the transpositions just mentioned is to avoid such instances.

The percussion player surrounded by a galaxy of instruments must sit some distance from his part, and might even have to play looking over his shoulder. His part needs to be written in a large enough hand to be seen under such conditions. Such is the percussionist's trust in his fellow players that he will always prefer a cue from another department of the orchestra; melodic cues are more easily found there anyway, but if a percussionist gets lost or makes a wrong entry it is more likely to be because of an ill-prepared part than a lack of ability.

Keyboard Instruments

The commonest of these within the orchestra are the piano, and its close relatives—celeste, harpsichord, etc. All use treble and bass clefs and are written on two staves, though the celeste, which sounds an octave higher than written, can often be accommodated on one stave only. The principle of one stave for each hand should be maintained where possible; when hands share a stave it is usually necessary to reverse the normal direction of stems. The use of an uncompleted bracket to show that notes written in one stave are to be played by the 'other' hand is usually superfluous. All instruments use key signatures. '8va' signs can be used freely above the stave though they are rarely necessary for the celeste and never for the harpsichord. '15ma' can be used for the piano, but can usually be avoided in a part; only the piano uses '8va bassa'.

Pedalling for the piano is often a matter for the performer, and need not be added unless something very specific is required. Some celestes have a sustaining pedal but the effect is minimal.

Good page turns are also essential for the pianist, though many printed orchestral piano parts seem to assume that the pianist has at least three hands. It is not possible to play the opening of Bartók's *Miraculous Mandarin*, for example, without losing some of the notes in a page turn; in this instance the loss is not likely to be noticed in the generally high dynamic level, but the turn in the middle of a solo is as much bad planning in a piano part as in any other.

Piano duet music in a score must be written with one part beneath the other, but, although it is time-consuming, it is better to lay out a part with each player's part on opposite facing pages; page turns must obviously be at the same point for each player, though either of them may turn the page.

For organ and harpsichord music, see p. 64.

Harp

In the remoter sharp keys it is better to write the enharmonic flat equivalents for the harp; double sharps and double flats simply do not exist on the harp, and any copyist encountering them should have no hesitation in renaming the notes. Harp pedalling, if thoroughly understood by the composer, may be written into the score; it is in fact a useful way of getting to understand the instrument's problems, and to avoid writing impossibilities. On the other hand, a few random indications of a change of pedalling are quite useless. Changes are usually written between the staves well in advance if possible; if they are to happen whilst playing then they should be written above. Of the many systems available, that of naming the notes in two tiers according to the layout of the pedals seems preferable. The copyist may also add the pedalling if he has a similar understanding, as if it is totally accurate (as it needs to be) it can save rehearsal time; on the other hand, the composer who said to me not long ago that 'harpists ought to be able to know how to play their instrument without additional advice' probably had a good point.

Good page turns are essential for the harp, and ideally rests should appear both at the foot of the old page and the top of the new; this is not always possible of course, but the shortening, for example, of five bars' rest into three empty ones followed by two with a cue written in, is a useful device for creating ideal conditions. Harp harmonics have already been discussed on p. 33.

Plucked Instruments

The guitar uses only the treble clef, though it sounds an octave lower than written; the true bass guitar, which also sounds an octave lower than written, uses both treble and bass clefs. Mandolin music is written as it sounds in the treble clef. Composers often ask for retuning of these instruments—the most usual being the lowering of the bottom guitar string to D.

In such cases it is not necessary to transpose the part to assist the player's fingering. Lute music should be laid out on two staves, but the copyist is advised to leave a line above each system in order that the player may add his own tablature notation. This and other similar symbolic notation for the guitar is best left as a mystery to all but the player.

Vocal Parts

The writing of vocal music has already been dealt with in Chapter 7. Unlike all other composite groups, the choir is considerably assisted by having a score of all voice parts in preference to individual lines only. The score can offer any amount of assistance with cueing and pitching of notes (for which there is no mechanical aid as with instruments); whereas an individual soprano part, for example, will give the sopranos a feeling of being isolated and lost. Instrumental cues are, of course, essential during any long passage of rest.

(See also p. 71.)

CHAPTER TWELVE

Random Music

The allowance of an increasing amount of freedom to the performer is becoming part of our modern musical language and a few notes on some of the notational devices now generally accepted are appropriate. For the most part, each individual composer seems to have evolved his own method of notation and this can even change from one work to the next. Nevertheless, some procedures are becoming more or less standardized and do not need to be accompanied by the lengthy verbal explanations which also seem to be becoming part of modern notation.

Rhythm

In using a random (free) technique the customary rhythmic notation is generally replaced by a more proportional one in which the exact rhythmic values are not implied, and do not in fact exist. Instead, the position of the notes on the page will suggest values and relationships, within a certain amount of confinement. This will be more easily understood from an example, but it is first necessary to appreciate slightly different, or additional, meanings of some standard symbols, as follows:

(a) ♪   a quick detached note.

(b) ♪ ♪♪   ♪   a group of quick detached notes,
                     separated by silences of relative
                     durations suggested by the spacing

(c)

as at (b) but the notes held for the duration suggested by both spacing and beam length. A stroke through the first stem and the beam 𝄏𝄏 would indicate as fast as possible.

(d)

as at (c) but notes of longer duration, though strictly speaking, there is virtually no difference between (c) and (d).

These four elements might be combined as follows:

Four irregular short notes (A) separated by silences (rests) of varying lengths are followed by a similar group (B) in which the notes are sustained until the next is sounded. (C) consists of two notes of a longer duration separated by a silence and immediately followed by a short detached note and another silence. (D) begins with a short detached note followed immediately by a long held note lasting to the end of the example.

In the previous example the actual sequence of notes is fixed; further randomness may be expressed as follows:

(e)

read from left to right, or right to left (and usually, start anywhere); furthermore, continue repeating for the duration of the wavy line. (The duration might also be expressed by the use of an extended beam, if appropriate, though this is less satis-factory; sometimes a group is meant to continue until the next written one, but this is best explained in a note to that effect.)

(f)

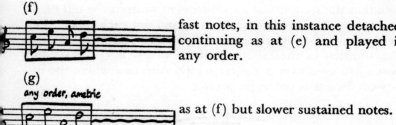

fast notes, in this instance detached, continuing as at (e) and played in any order.

(g)

any order, ametric

as at (f) but slower sustained notes.

Total unevenness in rhythm can be assured by the addition of the word 'ametric' above the box. The same principles of detached and sustained notes as in (a)–(d) above can of course be incorporated into (e)–(g).

Pitch

Approximate pitches may be noted in two ways:

(h) a random collection of notes, chords, and clusters, usually applied to an 'attack' on a keyboard instrument.

(i) very quick irregular pitches, in this case beginning in a high register and working down.

Independent rallentando and accelerando are written thus:

(j)

117

Note that the second and all subsequent beams arise out of, or close to, the main connecting beam, and not each other; they are drawn best by beginning at the denser end of the group. The addition of the falling or rising arrow is optional, and more often used over a shorter tempo variation where the use of many beams is not appropriate;

(k)

Tremolo

Various types of tremolo may be indicated as under:

(l) $\quad$ (m) $\quad$ (n)

(l) is an even level tremolo of the type usually indicated in normal rhythmic notation by a number of strokes through the stem; (m) increases or decreases in speed; (n) is level except for a sudden central rise and fall in speed. Many combinations are possible; for example, the following would indicate an increasing tremolo gradually involving more drums, with a final concluding stroke.

Although relative variations in the speed of tremolo are thus easily shown, differing requirements of speed related to the even tremolo are best expressed in words rather than density of stroke; thus (although it is a very rare refinement), the first version of the following is preferable.

One final 'innovation' which is really a variant of (e) is the following:

(o)

which, in simplest terms means 'follow the direction of the line (or any line)'; that is, play the first note, then select any one of the three on the second stem, then any one of two. Notes four and five are obligatory, followed by a further choice of three. An interesting application of this may be seen in Harrison Birtwistle's *Verses for Ensembles*.

I feel sure that these few 'new' principles are sufficient for a basic understanding of how to set down 'free' music. They should be readily understood by most practising musicians, (a claim which could not have been made even five years ago), and may be used without the need of further verbal explanation. They may all be extended, developed, added to, discarded, or rejected in favour of other methods. (Since they are used by more than one established composer, however, and have been shown to work, there is every reason for them to be adopted by others and continue to be used. How else are we to establish and stabilize any new necessary notation?)

The student composer drawn to this mode of composition will do well to remember that any notational device he invents or borrows from an unfamiliar source will need explanation, and any unnecessary complexity should be avoided if possible. As with standard notation, there is little point in placing a deliberately complex score before a performer if one hopes to get the best results. For some further study on the subject see the more recent works of Hans Werner Henze, Luciano Berio, and the more fully (musically) notated works of Karlheinz Stockhausen, whose *Zyklus* contains much of interest to anyone who can follow the unfortunate English of the instructions.

Scores

We have now reached the point at which we can consider the incorporation of freedom into a score. The first and perhaps the most difficult idea to accept is the almost total suspension of vertical alignment, which at best becomes merely approximate. In its simplest forms, randomness may be considered to fall into one of three categories; the sounds will either be totally freely produced (in concerted music, perhaps under a pause, or cancellation of metre), related to a time scale, or related to some other happening, such as another player reaching a given point in his part. Within these confines the exact placing of the notes is left to the performer; if there is more than one part it can be seen that the exact placing of notes of one part beneath those of another has no meaning.

The limits of the freedom need to be explained to the performer; that is, he must know not only what to play (even if he is allowed to choose it himself), but when to begin it and when to finish it. This might be anywhere at all, or related to a sign from a conductor, or some other element such as what another player is doing. The same example, laid out in different ways, will serve to illustrate these possibilities.

The notation used in the above score has already been explained: note that the use of rests is virtually unnecessary. The bar line here is included as a point of reorientation, where flute and bassoon commence new patterns simultaneously; the whole could be written as a single time-span using one of the methods which follow. Apart from this one point of unanimity it will be seen that no occurrence has an exact point of beginning or ending. An individual oboe part should be written thus:

Now a little more order will be imposed on the proceedings.

Here various instruments are asked to begin playing when others have reached definite points. The duration of the first bar is now governed by the actual events rather than the timed duration previously suggested, though the ultimate length of the second bar is still related to time. The oboe part will now be written thus:

In the following version, further order has been imposed by relating the events to a time scale.

The conductor gives a beat every second, and the players take their cues from this. Note that the fifth second is obviously included although nothing significant takes place here: although the conductor's beats are equal in time, they need not be equidistant on the page. We are now on the way back to a standard rhythmic notation, of course, and this particular system is often used in conjunction with simultaneous measured (barred) events. A point to remember in relating the two systems is that the bar line has no existence in time, and the passing seconds actually fall on the first note or beat of a bar not on the bar line. Thus (a) is correct in the following, whereas the often seen (b) is not.

The oboe part for this third version will be written as follows:

Note that all the passing seconds must be included, though those not related to an event in the actual oboe part are best bracketed.

An alternative to the previous method of governing the freedom is for the events still to be regulated by a conductor but giving signals to the players at non-regular intervals. In the following version it is only the conductor's musical interpretation which decides when the beats are given.

Again the oboist's part must show all the beats, whether they apply to his part or not.

Any combination of all the above methods is possible; for example, taking some beats from the conductor (timed or otherwise) and some from other players. In fact, any number of permutations is possible, but it is not my intention to stimulate ideas of composition, merely to suggest how they might be written down. The foregoing should provide sufficient basic knowledge to work from.

Accidentals

A warning is necessary on the use of accidentals in such passages; the system of accidentals applying only to the notes they precede must, if adopted, be rigidly maintained. It can, because it virtually disposes of the need for the natural sign, give rise to the following unfortunate passage, in which the seventh, eighth, ninth, eleventh, twelfth, fourteenth, and fifteenth notes are F natural.

To apply accidentals sometimes only to the notes they precede, sometimes to a phrase, and sometimes to a whole bar is simply bad musical grammar. (This sort of thing tends to arise from composing a short score or piano score, and using this as a copy for orchestrating, without due attention to the details.)

To avoid the endless, and pointless, repetition of accidentals in continuously repeating groups the modification of having accidentals applying only to the notes they precede, except where a note or group of notes is immediately repeated, is often met. This takes care of (a) below, but in (b) would seem to suggest that the last two notes are naturals; would any player sight-read them as such? And would not a few naturals help in (c)?

Unfortunately, there is no happy solution which will exactly satisfy complete pedantry, but here lies the answer. Absolute pedantry, even where possible in musical notation, is almost as unhelpful to the performer as inaccuracy; I would recommend the tempering of whatever method is adopted with a few additional helpful safety accidentals, at least at the sort of point at which the intelligent copyist feels that he himself might misread.

Although all of the foregoing might be regarded as simply touching on the question of random music, my only intention has been to detail some of the systems I feel are now readily understood by performers without further verbal explanation. It will not be difficult to discover much more which is only comprehensible when accompanied by pages of explanation (graphic music, for example), and sometimes not even then. However, I would not suggest that any notation that requires to be further explained with words is necessarily bad notation; it was not so very long ago that the now comparatively simple methods detailed in this chapter also needed explanation.

Tape

Though basically beyond the scope of this book, the frequent use of electronic tape in composition prompts me to make two recommendations. For an admirable way to notate the appearance and behaviour of a tape in a score Roberto Gerhard's *Collages* (Symphony 3), could not, I think, be improved on. This is of course a solution in its simplest form;

we are not told what is on the tape, but it does tell us when the tape is playing and at what volume and can consequently be used as a part for the operator to play from. At the other extreme, the minute detail included in Gottfried Koenig's *Electronische Studie II* leaves anyone with sufficient technical knowledge to understand it in no doubt whatsoever over the outcome.

CHAPTER THIRTEEN

Time-Saving and Time-Wasting

Checking

From the composer's point of view the act of producing a final manuscript is probably the most laborious and tedious of his tasks; creative work must be suspended whilst drudgery takes over. These moments can be quite revealing, however, and besides the always present temptation to make small changes it is not unusual for a number of practical details to present themselves to the observant composer. On the other hand, such details can equally be overlooked, and often are; I have recently come across instances of a player being required to play both E♭ and bass clarinet simultaneously, a percussionist being asked for a sudden six-note chord on the vibraphone and a retuning of three timpani in the space of about four seconds, and a bass clarinet being requested to double the ordinary B♭ clarinet at the unison, which would have meant playing several bars at least an octave beyond the top of the treble clef. Foolish errors indeed, which the composer should notice in preparing a copy of his score for others to work from.

Whoever has to write out the parts, when confronted with these problems, has three choices. One is to refer back to the composer; this is not always possible, and unless the problem involves a truly major decision, I have always tried to avoid this. Where a reasonably obvious solution is apparent, it would seem best to adopt this and make an independent note in the score for future reference. I would not advocate tampering freely with a composer's score, but often on presenting a query to a composer I have been met with equal uncertainty, and the offering of a *fait accompli* can solve the problem immediately.

The second possibility is merely to copy what is written; although I have seen this attitude adopted often, it seems to me to be an avoidance of responsibility. Putting a downright impossibility into a player's part is almost bound to waste future rehearsal time—I write 'almost' as I once copied a series of bottom Cs into a clarinettist's part, not realizing it until the rehearsal was under way. When that particular moment passed by without incident I asked the player concerned about the unplayable notes. 'Oh, it didn't seem worth querying; I just left it out', was the reply.

The third solution I have already presented in dealing with the first. Solving the problem oneself without reference to anyone is sometimes the only possible course when the music is required urgently for rehearsal or performance. If the work is likely to be performed again, of course, queries should be taken up as soon as possible; one finds that they often aren't. Scores and parts of quite a few standard works have had the same unsolved queries in them ever since their first airings.

(It should have become apparent that the value of the person who copied a work attending its rehearsal is considerable. Though his work is unlikely even to be noticed unless it is bad—a strange reward—he can well deal with queries on the spot that the conductor should not have to waste his time with.)

Short Cuts in Part-Writing

Some fairly common and accepted forms of saving time in writing scores have already been mentioned in Chapter 9. A score might contain any number of abbreviations (depending on for whom it is intended) and might even be a short score on just a few staves or even an annotated piano score for an independent orchestrator (a not uncommon practice in film music, for example). When one extracts a set of parts from a score there are also a number of devices varying in their degree of acceptability.

SHORT CUTS IN PART-WRITING

The use of repeat signs for a continually recurring phrase is the most common, though I must state a personal preference for the phrase being fully written out each time, with every appearance numbered. The phrase which crosses the bar line can rarely be asked for again by the use of the sign; there will nearly always be some detail of expression left uncomfortably hanging over. Although occasionally extreme haste may well demand it, the regular use of this symbol for repeats filling only a bar or less seems nothing short of idleness. Before resorting to the use of such a sign it should be considered whether the recurring phrase is one that can easily be retained in the memory whilst reading through lines of symbols.

In a large-scale work time can often be saved, in working through passages of rests only (or of very few notes), by using parts already copied as masters, rather than the score. If a long passage exists in a work in which, for example, the woodwind and brass are mostly silent, most of the parts will conform to an identical pattern. After copying one part from the score (probably the first flute) the remaining 'silent' parts can be copied from this. This process can save a considerable amount of time, as it eliminates any need for subsequent counting of empty bars, planning of layout, etc.

Three warnings about such a procedure are very necessary. Any copy to be used as a master in such a way must be most thoroughly checked; the carrying forward of even the smallest of errors into several other parts can be disastrous. Additionally only one master copy should be used as such; the temptation to copy second horn from first, third from second, fourth from third, and so on, must be firmly resisted. No matter how accurate the first copy is, the succeeding accumulation of errors can be quite surprising (and tiresome to correct). Secondly, a very thorough check is necessary to be certain that the appropriate instruments are truly silent or very inactive during the section covered by the master copy, and allowances made wherever needed; small details are very easily overlooked in this practice. The third warning concerns cueing, which there is almost certain to be during a long silent passage. Cues for all the instruments will not necessarily be the same (e.g., a cue leading in a first oboe would be superfluous for the second and third if they did not also play, though what the first oboe actually did play would well be cued into the second and third). Transposition of cues in parts for transposing instruments can also easily be forgotten.

It will be seen that this practice is only a true time-saver used over a fairly long passage; otherwise the individual plotting of each part is recommended.

Another time-saving method, or reputedly so, is the copying of 'double' wind parts—that is the first and second player's music on the same page. (There are rare instances where three parts can be accommodated on one copy if all three differ seldom and very little, but these are truly exceptional.) Let me at first say that, with very few exceptions, I feel this is a practice which should be discontinued. It is rarely the time-saver it is claimed to be, as the additional problems of layout and alignment usually take up most of any time saved in writing passages once only, having to plan only one part, etc. As far as the players are concerned, whilst I have never heard of anyone actually objecting to a double part, most would apparently prefer their own part only, subject to the considerations which follow.

The arguments for and against double parts may be summarized as follows. In favour: if the parts are fairly inactive, or both players play much in unison, copying time can be saved. Difficult music requiring interaction between the two players can be shown more helpfully—though here the single part with a good cue line is probably better. Normally a copy of a double part should be provided for each player, but it is possible for one part to be used by both players (any possible saving on reproduction costs is negligible, but this provision can cut down the number of music stands needed in an over-crowded orchestra pit, for example). And finally, if there is ever likely to be one or more instruments missing (as in a school orchestra or an amateur orchestra) it is possible for a single player to switch to the second part if necessary to complete the harmony or to provide a missing solo.

Against the providing of double parts are a number of factors, including the converse of much of the preceding paragraph. 'One part for one player' is a golden rule (with occasional modifications which have been suggested throughout this book). Active double parts are not time-saving to copy. Page turns come more often, and can be quite difficult to find—a rest in both parts is normally necessary, though one player can turn two separate copies in an emergency (a practice best avoided). If players share a copy the left-hand player will have difficulty reading the extreme right of the right-hand page, and vice versa (this is particularly true of the transverse flute player). Another problem not often realized is one of tessitura; first players play high notes, second players lower ones. This may sound ridiculously obvious, but it does mean that between the systems (staves two and three on a page, for example) a high part is written on a line beneath a low one, and sometimes the two can only be prevented from running together by leaving a line between systems. This reduces the number of systems per page, of course, which adds to any existing difficulties.

Two staves should always be used for double wind parts, unless both instruments have the same music, or one or both are resting. The simplest of independent parts may be combined on one stave if both parts have exactly the same rhythms, and all other indications are equal. Even so, it is often not easy for the second player in particular to read the lower part; separate stemming in such cases is essential, with the possible exception of on- and off-beat vamping in a not too fast tempo. The difficulty is intensified if players share a part.

Finally it seems to me that a great deal of time is wasted in trying to discover ways of saving time—or avoiding work. It is quite probable that familiar, tried, and proven methods are the best.

CHAPTER FOURTEEN

Checking and Proof-Reading

Anyone who writes down music may be called upon at some time to check and correct work, or even to read proofs. (One should never part with work without having at least checked to see that a copy has the same number of bars as the original; this takes so little time, and can ultimately save so much, that even the last-minute job should be treated in this way.)

Work for checking will be in one of two basic forms; one suitable for making corrections on, the other best left unmarked. In the first category come proofs from an engraver, usually printed in white on a green background, and consequently a little more difficult to read to the inexperienced eye; prints made from transparencies and similar reproductions; and top-copy prepared work from an autographer, covered by a transparent sheet on which corrections are marked. All of these can be marked directly.

In the other group come what might be described as top copies; ordinary copies made on opaque paper, original transparencies, etc. This group should not be marked at all, unless one is making the corrections in addition to discovering the errors. The light-coloured pencils often recommended for marking transparencies because they reputedly leave no trace on a print almost invariably do show in reproduction.

Corrections

Corrections to this last group need to be separately listed on a sheet ruled into columns for page, line, bar, and details of correction. This might initially seem tiresome, but it is far more valuable to the corrector (as opposed to checker) than a perhaps obscurely marked copy; the same corrector is also saved difficult and tricky work removing marks made by the checker.

Corrections to be made on copies in the first category mentioned above should be made at the actual point where the error occurs, ringed, and a line drawn from the ring to the margin where the correct version should be written again, together with any verbal description which may be thought additionally necessary. This will enable the corrector to locate errors without having to re-study the text, and also to check that the corrections have in fact been made.

Not all literary proof-reading correction symbols are suitable for music; for instance a symbolic instruction to insert a space may be confused with one to add a sharp. The musical slur and unwanted space are similar signs, as are the bass clef and printers' inversion sign. Two symbols are basic equipment, however; $\mathcal{L}$ signifying an insertion, and $\mathcal{G}$ requiring a deletion; these may be used freely, without fear of misunderstanding. Further investigation into the byways of printers' and publishers' rules may be made by reading Hart's *Rules for Compositors and Readers* (Oxford University Press) and a booklet, issued by Faber and Faber Ltd., entitled *Notes for Authors— Your MS and Your Proofs*.

Method

Checking should be carried out very systematically, with a deeply suspicious mind; one's approach to everything should be not 'is this correct?' but 'what is wrong with this?' Notes and rests on the page, together with modes of expression relating to them, can usually be checked together, but it is invariably necessary to check clefs, key and time signatures, marginal nomenclature (noting particularly consistency of abbreviations, etc.), tempo directions, and in fact all 'outside the stave' indications independently. Texts, with spelling, punctuation, and division of syllables, need special attention. Ties and slurs, and sometimes even phrases, often do not run from one system to the next when they should; a tied-over note with a slur appearing at the end of one page but not at the beginning of the next is a common error. Vertical alignment can only be checked as a separate duty; it is my experience that the engraver excels in this field, aligning simultaneous groups of four, seven, thirteen, and nineteen, for example, with an accuracy that leaves the autographer far behind and which an ordinary music-writer cannot hope to achieve. In this connection it should be borne in mind what standard of typographical accuracy is required for the particular work in question. Whilst an error as such cannot be passed in any copy, the standards of printed music cannot be expected to apply absolutely to manuscript. Pedantry is not necessarily desirable.

Composers rarely make the best proof-readers of their own work; apart from the sometimes irresistible temptation to make last-minute alterations, the mind invariably tends to suggest to the eye what it should be seeing, rather than the eye telling the mind what it does see.

When a score has been checked, and the parts are then copied from it, numerous additional errors are almost certain to be found. This rather frightening situation may serve to remind one of the exceptional care necessary in checking.

The following double example appears first with a number of errors worked into it (rather more, it is hoped, than would normally be found) and secondly with errors marked ready for correction.

Whatever the error it is never necessary to do more than make the correct version clear as simply as possible. Writing long messages in the margins to the copyist or compositor, calling him an idiot because he has written G instead of A (he wouldn't have done it deliberately), or filling the margins with exasperated comments, does nothing to assist in the making of a correction. In fact, antagonizing copyists can be a dangerous sport. Comments of the 'see previous page' type are also time-wasting, and often not sufficiently clear and detailed to enable a correction to be made properly.

Finally, in proofs the quality of the paper and density of the print are often inferior to what is intended in the final presentation; this need not cause any concern, but one must bear in mind that a paper fault might easily be mistaken for a staccato dot and vice versa.

Conclusion

Many times during the writing of this book I have felt that none of it could really be necessary, and the whole content must surely be common knowledge for anyone putting music on paper. Then along would come a manuscript for working on, which proved that it was by no means common knowledge; this continuing circumstance (and the patient encouraging nudging of my publisher) is the main reason for the book. It is my hope that it will help students, scholars, teachers, and even perhaps some professional composers and copyists—in fact, anyone who ever needs to write down music.

For those interested in greater details than I have thought it necessary to present here—and that should surely be all of us—a short list of useful reference books is included. The voracious reader will find points of dissent between us all; perhaps that suggests the need for more uniformity in notational practice.

Useful Reference Books

Apel, Willi: *The Notation of Polyphonic Music, 900–1600* (Mediaeval Academy of America, 1961).

Boehm, Laszlo: *Modern Music Notation* (G. Schirmer Inc., New York, 1961).

Copland, Aaron: *On the Notation of Rhythm* (League of Composers, New York, 1944).

Donato, Anthony: *Preparing Music Manuscript* (Prentice Hall Inc., New Jersey, 1963).

Hart, Horace: *Rules for Compositors and Readers* (Oxford University Press, London, 1967).

Karkoschka, Erhard: *Notation in New Music* (English translation by Ruth Koenig) (Universal Edition Ltd., London, 1972).

Parrish, Carl: *The Notation of Mediaeval Music* (Faber & Faber, London, 1958).

Read, Gardner: *Music Notation. A Manual of Modern Practice* (Allyn & Bacon Inc., Boston, 1964).

Rosenthal, Carl A.: *Practical Guide to Music Notation* (MCA Music, New York, 1967).

Stone, Kurt: *Problems and Methods of Notation* (Princeton University Press, 1963).

Whitman, George: *Introduction to Microtonal Music* (British & Continental Music, London, 1970).

Notes for Authors—Your MS and Your Proofs (Faber & Faber, London, 1969).

DATE DUE